TREE OF SAPPHIRES

TREE *of* SAPPHIRES

THE ENLIGHTENED QABALAH

DAVID GODDARD

WEISERBOOKS
Boston, MA/York Beach, ME

First published in 2004 by
Red Wheel/Weiser, LLC
York Beach, ME
With offices at:
368 Congress Street
Boston, MA 02210
www.redwheelweiser.com

Library of Congress Cataloging-in-Publication Data
Goddard, David.
Tree of sapphires : the enlightened Qabalah / David Goddard.
p. cm.
Includes bibliographical references.
ISBN 1-57863-303-6
1. Cabala. I. Title.
BF1623.C2G64 2004
135'.47--dc22
2004008052

Typeset in Minion and Univers by Kathryn Sky-Peck
Printed in Canada
TCP
11 10 09 08 07 06 05 04
8 7 6 5 4 3 2 1

Respectfully dedicated to
Z'ev ben Shimon Halevi,
the Chariot of Da'ath,
a Teacher of teachers

CONTENTS

THE TREE OF SAPPHIRES

The Tree of Life was withheld from Adam and Eve, when by
*   eating of Knowledge's fruit; they fell into duality.*
Chaldean winged spirits guard this Tree of Life, while Egyptian
*   Thoth writes upon each leaf.*
From this blazing, unconsumed Tree, Metatron instructs Moses
*   in unity.*
Beneath this Tree, Deborah and the high priestesses prophesy.
Odin hangs upon this World-Tree, gaining the Runes of Wisdom.
Within its trunk Osiris sleeps, yet will he wake to eternal life.
Jesus is still nailed to this Tree, with rose-thorns about his brow.
Canopied by this same Tree, Siddartha awakens as a Buddha.
And from this Wish-fulfilling Tree, alchemical Sages harvest the
*   golden Fruit of Immortality.*

                                                —D. G.

INTRODUCTION

I have often been asked: Is Qabalah a religion? It is not. Qabalah is a spiritual tradition. Religion and spirituality are not the same thing. Religion is a means to get to a certain state of knowing—*gnosis*. Spirituality is the state you are in when you get there. A spiritual practitioner is one who has come to know the realities that religious scripture and imagery indicate—directly, if imperfectly. The knowledge is imperfect because it involves realities that transcend form and dualistic thinking.

This is very important to grasp. Religious image and scripture are metaphorical not literal; they need to be perceived wisely as poetic allegory, not as concrete fact. All religions, without exception, are time-fettered attempts to communicate with (and label) the inexpressible. Once you grasp this, you automatically move into a stance where you look for what you have in common with other religious expressions. If, however, you read your own religion as "prose" instead of as poetry, you automatically demonize others whose religious images conflict with your own deeply held beliefs.

We see this in the ongoing conflict in the Middle East, where three world religions—Judaism, Christianity, and Islam (all derived from

Abraham)—cannot tolerate one another because they each have different names and myths for the same deity. In the 21st century, it is time we outgrew such things. Such views cannot help us realize the Transcendent Mystery for which the term "God" is a metaphor.

A realized spiritual practitioner can worship with other people in any setting—synagogue, church, mosque, temple, or grove—because they have learned to be conscious of the Divine in all places and in all beings. This is represented by the esoteric aphorism that teaches, "Mock not the name by which another knows God."

Skillfully applied, religion can be useful to spiritual practitioners by helping them communicate with others who use the same imagery or share the same associations. But we need not be bound by its practices. We choose it only because it is helpful. As with any tool, when it has done the job, we lay it aside. Or we may retain it for its inherent beauty, like a picture or a piece of music we personally find inspiring. The important thing is that we not impose our preferences on others or judge them by whether they like or dislike that picture or piece of music. Having "tasted" the One Reality, the truly spiritual person is no longer attached to religion, but rather sees it for what it is and continues forward to actualize that which religion can only suggest.

To be real spiritual practitioners—authentic Qabalists—we must transcend all traces of sectarianism and religious exclusivity and rise to a recognition that all who serve the Absolute are our companions. For they too are on the journey to Jerusalem Above—the Mother of us all, where, it has been said, there are many mansions.

A true Qabalist is one who receives enlightenment from Above, one whose eyes are open to the One Light and whose ears are open to receive from those-who-know. A true Qabalist gains knowledge, not from those who preach, speculate, or theorize, but from those who have realized the unity that alone is Eternal. The eternity they seek is beyond all form, name, or definition. It transcends all things, births all things. It is the deepest identity that dwells within all beings. It is that which those-who-know have called the Supreme Rapture.

Another question I am often asked is: Why use Qabalah in esoteric work, why not some other system? Isn't it just a matter of personal preference or bias? Again the answer is no. Qabalah is taught by most of the esoteric schools of the West because its purity and common sense form the best foundation for all subsequent work. Its philosophy and techniques underpin the entire structure of the Western esoteric tradition. Moreover, in its practical aspect, alchemy, the Qabalah also offers the means to reach the highest attainments of spiritual illumination.

The reason why the Qabalah holds the preeminent position it does in the mystical and occult traditions lies in one simple fact: the Qabalah is the only *complete* esoteric system to have survived in the West.

A real spiritual tradition is able to give its practitioners the means to achieve mental and emotional poise, psychological maturation, spiritual awareness, and self-transcendence. In short, it must be able to guide the individual, stage by stage, to enlightenment. Christine Hartley wrote,

> All mystery systems, all metaphysical philosophy . . . are nothing more or less than systems of props whose sole object is to support and steady the human mind while it slowly prepares itself for the final plunge into Thrice Greatest Darkness, which is the Ineffable Light, which is in very truth, Nirvana—At-one-ness with the Supreme Life.[1]

An authentic tradition is a complete system of valid metaphysics. It has a complete cosmology that is both observable and experiential. It needs to teach emanation and numeration in order to give the sequence and frequencies that constitute interdependent existence. It requires a profound understanding of the nature of awareness and the interior constitution. It must possess a storehouse of images that are embedded within the collective unconscious and provide an array of meditative techniques in both creative and formless modes. It must be adept in true education (literally, "to bring forth") of both the conscious and subconscious aspects of the mind. And with all this, it must also be able to transmit to the prepared the art of integration and skillful application to produce gradual and sustainable transformation.

Of the great Mystery schools of the Mediterranean basin—the temples of Egypt, the Greek cults of Eleusis and Orpheus, the school of Pythagoras, or the Hermetic wisdom of Alexandria—none have survived in their entirety. There are some bare bones remaining, but the living organism—the "Body of Light"—is lost to us. We do not possess the complete system necessary to journey all the way to the mountaintop. This is the quintessential reason why the mystics and adepts of the West practice Qabalah. It has preserved the philosophy, the words of power (the mantras) and methods of the ancient Mysteries. For example, in Dion Fortune's esoteric novel, *Moon Magic*, we read how a modern adept of the Western Tradition invokes the ancient Egyptian deity, Isis:

> The high full-moon in the mid-heavens shines clear,
> Oh hear the invoking words, hear and appear!
> Shaddai-El-Chai and Rhea, Binah, Ge -,[2]

Shaddai El-Chai—the Almighty God of Life—is the Hebrew title for the Divine manifesting in the sephira of Yesod. The point is that we don't actually know the invoking words by which the adepts of ancient

4

Egypt called on Isis (itself a Greek noun for the Egyptian *Aset*) they are lost. The Qabalah imparts the Primordial Wisdom Tradition in imagery and language native to Western culture and experience. And most important, it is complete.

It is not the purpose of this book to give a detailed history of the Qabalah; that can be gleaned from the many available books (see Recommended Readings). This book has been written so you can learn to transmute the Qabalistic Tree of Life from an exterior diagram into an interior reality. Its purpose is to instruct you in the working methods of the Qabalah as practiced in the esoteric tradition. These methods, aptly described as the yoga of the West, are transformative by nature. If faithfully followed, they will extend your range of consciousness, deepen your perceptions, and give you first-hand knowledge of the purpose of existence and of your place in the Great Design.

It may, however, be useful to begin with a brief outline of the Qabalah as an esoteric tradition. As many readers will know, the Qabalah is, among other things, the mystical tradition of Judaism. It also forms the secret heart of Christianity (Rosicrucianism) and of Islam (Sufism). As such, the Qabalah is the common heritage of all People of the Book and it has deeply influenced Western culture as a whole. Since the Magic of Light is practical mysticism, Qabalah is the foundation of Western occultism as well.

In the Bible, the principal Qabalistic books of the Old Testament are Genesis, Exodus, Ezekiel, and Daniel; and in the New Testament, the Apocalypse (the Book of Revelation). The Qabalah was the treasure trove of the sages of Israel, particularly after the destruction of the temple and the Diaspora. It formed the basis for the spiritual regeneration of the Jewish religion through the *Baal-Shem-Tov* and the early Hasidic masters. It was the inspiration behind the spiritual impulse of the Renaissance, seen in the works of Marsilio Ficino, Ramon Lull, and Pico della Mirandola. It informed the mysticism of Teresa of Avila and John of the Cross, and Ignatius of Loyola (who founded the Jesuits) employed some of its methods. Its "ascension method" was employed by Mohammed to receive the Koran, and Qabalistic influence is seen in the teachings of the great Sufi masters, particularly Rumi.

In the European esoteric movement, Qabalah forms the basis of Rosicrucianism; the founders of Freemasonry employed its symbolism in their higher degrees, and the alchemists used it as the key to unlock the mystical techniques that comprised their *praxis*. In the last 130 years, the most influential Western esoteric teachers—Eliphas Levi, Paul Foster Case, Dion Fortune, W. E. Butler, Z'ev ben Shimon Halevi, and Gareth Knight—have all been practicing Qabalists.

Many think that the Qabalah is totally Judaic in origin; this is not correct. Qabalah no more belongs to the Jews than Buddhism does to the Tibetans or Christianity to the Vatican. No one people or any single individual can own a spiritual teaching. Of course, the Jewish mystics did culturally imprint the Qabalah; it wouldn't have worked for them if they had not. The same thing happened to Buddhism after it was brought to Tibet from India. This has always been the way of true esoteric work: adaptation to the culture and the times. In Jewish legend, it is said that the Qabalah was bought to Earth by the Archangel Ratziel, just after the death of Adam (thus long predating the birth of Abraham) to show us the way back to the Garden of Eden. Naturally, we pay respect to the sages of Israel because they preserved the Qabalah despite unimaginable odds. Similarly, the monasteries of Tibet preserved scriptures and teachings that would otherwise have been lost to the world. Nevertheless, the holy Qabalah is a message from divinity to all humanity.

Some of the Qabalistic philosophy is Chaldean and ancient Egyptian in origin—not too surprising a result when a nomadic people become exposed to the influence of a sophisticated and religious civilization. For example, the confirmative word "Amen" (a title of Kether, the first of the sphere of the Tree of Life) is derived from the name of the Egyptian god Amun, and is one of the most important technical terms in the Qabalah. Qabalistic angelology came mainly from the magi of Chaldea (during the Babylonian Captivity), as did the Script of Flame, the Hebrew alphabet. Later, Hellenistic Neoplatonism further influenced the Qabalah in Alexandria. The Qabalah is thus a precious repository for many streams of the ageless wisdom.

A spiritual tradition is a tapestry woven from many colored threads: revelation, history, culture, crisis, and reformation. All of these factors influence and develop a tradition. There is no such a thing as a *pure* tradition. From the moment an individual becomes part of a tradition, that person undergoes subtle changes and so does the tradition itself. In fact, an esoteric tradition must change and evolve if it is to remain an open channel for the influx of grace from the upper worlds. The moment a tradition ceases to change, it begins to stagnate and runs the risk of becoming an empty shell devoid of life. This also applies to the schools, orders, and groups that constitute a tradition. And, of course, this also applies to us as individual beings. When we cut ourselves off from the universal life, we freeze, atrophy, and eventually die. This can occur on all levels of our being: physical, emotional, mental, or spiritual.

The great creative power of which we are expressions is a living force that constantly seeks more perfect vessels through which to express itself as form. This thrust is the cosmic dynamic behind creation and evolution in the manifest universe, because eternity is in love with the forms of time. Force needs a form through which to work, for force without form is diffused and wasted. Likewise, form without a force is impotent. To invoke the right force into the correctly built form is the work of true initiates.

There are many streams that make up the great river that is the tradition of the holy Qabalah: the scholarly Rabbinic School, the ecstatic methods of the Hassidic and Ethiopian streams, the wisdom approach of the Toledo School, the redemptive mysticism of the Lurianic School, and the synthetic methods employed in the Alchemical Qabalah, which, as Dion Fortune pointed out, is the correct name for the form of Qabalah used in the Western Mystery Tradition.

I refer to the Alchemical Qabalah of the West as synthetic because it is a synthesis of several streams. This Alchemical Qabalah was formulated in Alexandria by a great school of initiates based in that Hellenistic capital of Egypt. Alexandria was the meeting place of all peoples in the ancient world and the great center of all learning for nearly a thousand years. In Alexandria, various spiritual traditions met and cross-fertilized each other: Greek Neoplatonism, Hebrew mysticism, Mahayana Buddhist tantras, Hindu Vedanta, Christian Gnosticism, and the wisdom of the indigenous Egyptian temples. The Alexandrian School of the Soul was responsible for the formulation of a spiritual impulse that, thanks to the Roman Empire, was spread throughout the Mediterranean basin, and into Europe, the Middle East, and North Africa. The Alexandrian School reformulated the ageless wisdom into a synthesis that wove those wisdom teachings together, forming the Alchemical Qabalah.

This synthesis made the Qabalah of the West strong in its spiritual armory and rich in its mystical treasury. It has inherited many formulae and techniques that make it versatile and adaptable to most life situations and conditions. It is now studied and practiced all over the world. Its roots draw from the primordial past, but it has proven throughout history its adaptability and its power to give to successive generations first-hand knowledge of the levels of existence. The Qabalah is a tried and tested way by which dedicated men and women may grow into their full potential as consciously eternal and immortal beings. This Alchemical Qabalah has been inherited from past teachers and is now imparted again, so that its life-affirming teachings and transformative methods may continue to assist others upon the Path of Return.

IN THE BEGINNING ...

Speak of the Qabalah and the Angels draw nigh.

The word *Qabalah* comes from a Hebrew verb meaning "to receive," as distinct from *Massorah*, meaning "tradition." The holy Qabalah, "the Reception," forms the basis of the Western esoteric path. To receive indicates a transmission of knowledge from mouth to ear, from teacher to pupil; but it also implies the concept of receiving, through your subtle senses, knowledge from the worlds above. Until you can and do receive instruction from those-who-know, from the communion of saints, you are a student of Qabalah, not a Qabalist. To become a true Qabalist, you must undertake the Work.

The Work

The acquisition of any skill, craft, or art requires self-disciplined practice, and this needs to come from within yourself, not from an external teacher or school. To become a Qabalist, you must develop your self-motivation and determination. Rest secure in the knowledge that, since others have attained spiritual growth by treading the way of Qabalah, you too can attain it if you apply yourself.

In the old language of the building guilds, there are three stages: Apprentice, Journeyman, and Craftsman. Apprentices are those who are accepted to learn from a Craftsman the basic skills of the trade and to assist in specialized projects. Journeymen have gained proficiency in all the basic theoretical skills and are now able to undertake work of their own, but still need to acquire the special skills that only experience can give. Craftsmen are adept (skillful) in their field, having mastered all aspects of theory and practice, and are able to instruct others. Although these terms are "time-fettered," what they signify is as valid today as in times past. Indeed, there is no such a thing as a "self-taught" Qabalist or esotericist, any more than there is a "self-taught" brain surgeon.

The Qabalah, and occultism in general, has a dubious reputation, and in some cases, rightly so. In this, it is similar to the martial arts, where many students profess that they only wish to learn the art for self-defense and discipline, but in fact use it to compensate for their own feelings of inadequacy. This rightly gives many martial arts a poor reputation, particularly among law-enforcement agencies. This is not a complete picture, however. There are thousands of dedicated, hard-working women and men all over the world for whom a martial art is a valid means of self-unfoldment and, in many instances, a spiritual path as well.

The esoteric tradition of the West—of which Qabalah is the core—is the same. It is the ego-centered and often delusional so-called "occultists" who draw the most attention to themselves and so bring disrepute to what is, in truth, a sacred science and a royal art—what the ancient sages called the Mysteries.

The term "Mysteries" is used here in the same sense that Catholic theologians use it—to refer to a spiritual reality that transcends normal reason. This doesn't mean the Mysteries are unreasonable; they are not, but they *do* transcend ordinary states of consciousness. Consequently, developing higher states of consciousness is an important part of esoteric training. The Qabalah teaches methods that enable you to enter these higher states. This initially requires the development of your mind, chiefly its faculties of attentiveness, visualization, and retention (also called concentration, imagination, and memory). In this book, you will use tried-and-tested means to develop your mental capacities in such a way that the process has transformative effects. In short, this is a form of energetic dynamics, a Western yoga. Once these basic building blocks are in place, you can begin your work in the upper worlds.

To be a true Qabalist, one worthy of the name, you must manifest what you learn in the higher worlds here on Earth, in your life and through your thoughts, words, and actions. This is why the Qabalah is also called the Work of Unification. And this is how you play your part in the evolution of all beings: by working on your soul and so becoming an effective tool for spirit. In the terminology of the guilds, the Apprentice is taught about the way and receives a map and letters of introduction. The Journeyman travels those inner realms and receives instruction direct from the inner teachers. But the Craftsman actually embodies the beauties of the spirit within his or her own being, manifesting heaven upon Earth.

The Work consists of several basic practices. Let's explore them and the reasons why we employ them in the Work.

BASIC MEDITATION TECHNIQUE

Your daily meditations should initially last for approximately fifteen minutes. On some occasions, this may seem too short a time, and at others, it may feel an eternity. This is because, when you are in inner space working on the inner planes, time (and space) is measured in states of consciousness and by the transition between those states. This same phenomenon occurs in ceremonial work. At first, it is helpful to have a clock in your meditation area to prevent you from acquiring extreme "time habits."

During meditation, outside noises may be distracting at first. To overcome this, make a firm intention to allow outside noises to pass through you unimpeded, offering them no mental resistance. Just allow the noises to flow through you. When you have gained experience, you will find that noise has little power to distract you.

MEDITATION POSTURE

The posture you should adopt for your meditation resembles that of the statues of the gods and pharaohs of Egypt.

1. Sit on a stool or straight-backed chair, your chin slightly inclined toward the chest, your neck vertebrae straight (trained dancers habitually carry their heads in this manner).

2. Your thighs should be parallel to the floor, your calves vertical, and your stockinged or bare feet firmly planted on the floor.

3. Place your elbows at right angles, with your hands resting lightly on your thighs. There should be no undue strain on any of your muscles.

This posture allows the forces contacted in meditation to flow freely throughout your body and your aura, uniting Above with Below. In the Western Mysteries, meditation postures that involve the crossing of legs or arms are used in specialized work of a particular nature.

RELAXATION TECHNIQUE

The ability to relax at will is essential for interior work. All meditations should be preceded by relaxation. At first, this takes some time, but practice will increase your skill. Relaxation makes your body a clear channel, transparent to the inflowing light, and enables energy to flow unimpeded.

1. When seated in your meditation posture, first focus upon your feet, then tense the muscles of both feet for about four seconds. Then allow them to relax.

2. Next, focus on the calves of your legs: tense, hold, then relax.

3. Continue this process upward through your entire body: thighs, buttocks, abdomen, chest, hands, forearms, upper arms, shoulders, and neck.

4. Tense your facial muscles and scalp by "pulling a face," holding it for four seconds, then relaxing the muscles.

This flexing and relaxing of muscles frees pockets of energy that become trapped by tension. Upon completion of a relaxation exercise, your body will feel united and poised.

THE 4:2:4 BREATH CYCLE

Breathing is an important way to absorb radiant energy. It is the primal movement. You are constantly breathing; it is an automatic process under the control of your subconscious mind (as are all body processes), yet it can also be directed from the self-conscious level. By inhalation, you absorb *prana*, (*ruach* in Hebrew), vitalizing energy. When you exhale, this energy is distributed through your physical body via the bloodstream. To use this energy to its fullest extent, you must breathe correctly. This does not mean that you have to walk around all day focused on your breathing. (In fact; that would be detrimental). It does mean that, during your meditation sessions, you should establish good breathing. Your subconscious will take it from there.

Another reason to establish the practice of deep breathing during meditation is to prepare for advanced work. During meditation at deep levels, trance, and astral projection, you tend to breathe shallowly. If this continues for a prolonged period, a projection can easily be broken. By making it a habit to breathe deeply each time you prepare to meditate, you build an automatic habit that will stand you in good stead later.

To obtain the maximum benefit from the air, you must breathe from the diaphragm—a muscle situated below your rib cage in your abdomen. Remember, you do not have to pull in the breath; atmospheric pressure will take care of that. Simply push out your diaphragm; your rib cage will expand and air will rush into your lungs. Please do not make the mistake of trying any forcible expansion of your chest. This can cause damage to fine blood vessels there. Let the muscles below your ribs do most of the work. If you do it properly, you will feel the expansion in the small of your back and at your sides, as well as in the front of your body. You should always try to ensure that you commence any cycle of conscious breathing by first contracting your diaphragm to expel the old, tired air from the bottom of your lungs.

1. Contract your diaphragm to empty your lungs of stale air;

2. Expand your diaphragm;

3. Inhale deeply to a count of four;

4. Hold your breath for a count of two;

5. Exhale completely to a count of four.

The pace of this number count should be your own, matched to your own lungs' capacity. Another person's breath cycle may be quicker or slower than your own. Listen to your breath cycle; it should be almost inaudible. If your breath cycle is noisy, it is not being performed correctly. The remedy is to slow the cycle down.

Once you are seated for meditation, establish this 4:2:4 breath cycle. When you have done it consciously for ten full cycles, dismiss it from your mind and move on to the next phase of your meditation.

THE QABALISTIC CROSS

All meditation should be preceded by a sealing of your subjective "sphere of sensation"—your aura. This helps you center down and focus exclusively on the work at hand. It aligns the meditation to the Divine. In the Western Mystery Tradition, the sealing of your aura is usually done using a formula called The Qabalistic Cross. Like all esoteric techniques, this formula has various applications and gradations of energy. At this point, it is important to free your mind from a superstitious belief that esoteric formulae in and of themselves are magical. They are not. Consciousness itself is the true magician. Formulae are tools that a trained mind employs. A hammer has no ability to affect anything unless taken up by a hand. In the same way, a formula is used as a focus for the mind to achieve a change in consciousness. Once that shift in consciousness is stabilized—when you can enter into it at will—the formula becomes redundant. This applies to all the apparatus of the Magic of Light: wands, swords, robes, temples. It is essential that you grasp this, because the purpose of the Mysteries is to enable you to transcend your limitations, not to exchange one set of chains for another.

It is true, however, that certain ancient formulae contain some inherent energy. This is because trained minds have used them as points of focus over long periods of time. But the successful use of even these archaic formulae is still dependent upon your being able to reproduce in yourself the states of consciousness that they represent. This is the underlying reason why untrained people, experimenting with esotericism, get "hit or miss" results. Remember: A magical formula is just that—a form, empty in itself until you empower it. This is why all the formulae and exercises given in this book teach both the inner and outer aspects.

1. Standing upright, visualize above your head an infinite expanse of radiant white light.

2. Visualize the sea of light concentrate itself into a brilliant sphere, shining about eight inches above your head.

3. Raising your right hand to touch your forehead, say: *ATEH.*

18

4. Point your right hand to your feet, imaging a line of white light descending from the sphere overhead, passing through your body, and forming a white sphere that encompasses your feet and ankles. Then say: *MALKUTH.*

5. Point to your right shoulder, seeing the brilliance moving to that shoulder, and say: *VE GEVURAH.*

6. Point to your left shoulder, seeing the brilliance moving with your hand across from your right shoulder to your left, and say: *VE GEDULAH.*

7. Cup both hands in front of your heart, saying: *LE OLHAM.*

8. Visualize once more the sphere of white brilliance above your head, and conclude by saying: *AMEN.*

You have now brought the energy of the Limitless Light into all your bodies (mental, astral, etheric, and physical). Feel yourself as expanded in size, with a blazing cross of light as the axis and expanse of your being. Rest for a while in that awareness. When your meditation session is complete, use the Qabalistic Cross again to seal the energies into the cells of your physical body.

The symbol used in the Qabalistic Cross does not represent the cross upon which Jesus was crucified. It is the Cross of Shabbathai, taken from the Qabalistic book *Sepher-Yetzirah*, the *Book of Formation*. Shabbathai is the Hebrew name for the planet Saturn, the finitizing principle in the universe. It is related to the teaching held by all traditions of the ageless wisdom, which affirms that the Divine dwells within every being: "There is none but He." In the poetic language of *Sepher-Yetzirah*, the Hebrew letter assigned to Saturn (*Tau*) is the "palace of holiness in the midst, sustaining all things." The point where the arms of the Qabalistic Cross intersect indicates the dwelling of the All-Good within the temple of the human body, teaching us that the Beloved resides in our heart-of-hearts forever. This is why, when you come to this part of the Qabalistic Cross, you cup your hands before your heart—to represent a lamp within which shines the Divine light—and say *le Olham*, here translated as "forever" or "unto eternity."

SALUTATIONS

The Sun, the star about which our planet orbits, is the physical body of an archangelic being of cosmic stature and degree. The aura of this being extends throughout our entire solar system. This being is sometimes called the Solar Logos. The planets in our solar system may be thought of as the chakras—the centers of force—of the Solar Logos. The Sun is the center of life and light that upholds all terrestrial manifestation. Everything we see and touch upon this planet is an adaptation of solar energy. The Sun grows all incarnate life. Our planet was born from the heart of the Sun and still contains within its center the "seed of the Sun," the molten core that holds titanic physical and spiritual forces.

The Sun is the crown of our solar system because it mediates the universal radiant energy into it. For this reason, many of the gods of ancient Egypt are crowned with Sun-disks. The ancient Mystery priesthoods of the classical pagan world wisely worshipped the Sun as the visible symbol of the Most High.

In the ancient temples of the Mysteries, the two most important daily rituals took place at dawn and at sunset. At high noon, the time of greatest light, consciousness was raised to the Solar Logos and its influence drawn down and married to the Earth.

The practice of turning to the Sun in consciousness is called a salutation. The Triple Salutations were practiced by the great Hermetic sages of Alexandria, and they have formed part of the daily discipline ever since. This does not mean that you have to get up at dawn every day; the practice is to perform the Morning Salutation (after ablutions) at the beginning of your day. Nor should you make a pious show of the salutations. They can be performed entirely mentally. They are not lengthy; they consist of brief but intense acknowledgments of the source of life and of our place in the great dance of the stars. When the Mid-day Salutation is given, since it is the time of greatest light, the key ideas you hold are: God made manifest in nature, the Sun as the visible crown of the physical plane, and aspiration to the Elder Brethren (the Masters of Service). When you have mentally aligned yourself with these sacred powers, you invoke peace upon all beings. After each salutation, perform the Qabalistic Cross (see page 17).

The Morning Salutation is as follows:

Hail to thee, the eternal One Reality, in whom we live and move and have our being forever; whose visible symbol of Shemesh now rises in the heavens. Hail unto thee Adon-Olham, Lord of the Universe, hail unto thee from the abodes of the morning.

The Mid-day Salutation is as follows:

Hail to thee, the eternal One Reality, in whom we live and move and have our being forever; whose visible symbol of Shemesh now shines at high heaven. Hail unto thee Adon-Olham, Lord of the Universe, hail unto thee from the abodes of the noonday.

There is an international network of people from all traditions who, at midday (local time), individually send up an invocation for world peace. So I add to my Mid-day Salutation the intercession: *May Adonai bless the nations with shalom.* I earnestly encourage everyone to avail themselves of this opportunity to be of service, in the Noon Network.

The Evening Salutation is as follows:

Hail to thee, the eternal One Reality, in whom we live and move and have our being forever; whose visible symbol of Shemesh now rises in the heavens. Hail unto thee Adon-Olham, Lord of the Universe, hail unto thee from the abodes of the evening.

Shemesh is the Hebrew name for our Sun. The ancient Egyptians called it the Star of Life. *Adon-Olham* is Lord of the Universe.

Victorian scholars, commenting on the *Corpus Hermeticum*, came to the (erroneous) conclusion that the only ceremonial observed by the Hermetic initiates of the Graeco-Egyptian period were the Salutations. This was mainly based on the scholars' romantic view that these philosophers (originally a title of the *mystae* and alchemists) were stoics and minimalists. In fact, the Hermetic philosophers performed the Salutations (which is where Alchemical Qabalah got them) in addition to the rites of the Mystery cults into which they were initiated.[3]

Keeping a Journal

You will find it invaluable to keep a diary of your meditations, ceremonies, and realizations. In it, note the times you performed your meditations and Salutations, and also when you omitted them. Like all self-disciplined tasks, at first you may be prone to forget from time to time, but with frequent practice, you will soon make this an integral part of your life. The Salutations build in you the habit of regularly rising in the transpersonal level of consciousness, into the overview of spirit.

THE FIRE FROM HEAVEN

There is only One Light,
And "you" and "me"
Are holes in the lamp-shade.

—MAHMUD SHABISTARI

In this chapter, we will continue to look at the basic practices employed in the Mysteries. Some of these may appear as child's play or seem too simple. But you must remember that the subconscious mind—which is the magical agent—thinks in images, and that most esoteric practice aims at engaging the subconscious. Without this engagement, esoteric study becomes mere intellectual speculation—interesting perhaps in itself, but no more able to effect changes in consciousness (let alone transformation) than any other area of academic metaphysics. In fact, the old alchemists often referred to the academic approach as the "false tincture," and to their Great Work as "child's play." But here again, you must remember that, when the sages write simply, they are being most subtle: "Unless ye become as little children ye shall not enter the Kingdom of Heaven." The *Malkuth ha' Shamain*, or the Kingdom of

Heaven, is a technical Qabalistic term for the state of consciousness necessary to enter the company of the illumined ones. No intellectual achievement, no learned metaphysics, no material status can gain entry to this august group. The only entry permit is to become as a little child, a creature of wonder and trust. Simple . . . ?

The Power of Sleep

Sleep is an activity little understood by those outside of practical occultism. Much of the advanced work of adepts takes place during sleep. Put briefly, during sleep, your consciousness withdraws from your physical body—just as you lay aside your clothes—and refocuses its awareness upon the inner planes. In its absence, your subconscious works to maintain and repair your body. A high proportion of the cells of your physical body are replaced in a twenty-four-hour cycle. Your subconscious also processes the experiences of its absentee landlord—your self-consciousness—as dreams.

Anything to which you give concentrated attention is impressed upon your subconscious mind and acts as instructions to it. Your subconscious then acts on those instructions and begins the process of bringing them into manifestation. This is the key to magic. It follows, then, that anything to which you give frequent or prolonged attention makes a greater impression upon the mirror of your subconscious mind than things to which you give little or fleeting attention. In magical training, you utilize this fact by performing regular daily meditations and practices, that place potent and transformative instructions into your subconscious mind.

Much of the early training in the Mysteries is concerned with transforming the images in your subconscious. We all have negative patterns resulting from images we built in our formative years. These potent images are instilled by our early experiences by parental and educational systems (not all of which are bad by any means), and by social pressures designed to keep us in our place and ensure that we conform to the herd-mind and accept religious and political authorities, preferably without question. Such negative images give rise to life-patterns of inadequacy, self-guilt, and the belief that we are somehow undeserving and unlovable. The force of these patterns, embedded as they are in the subconscious aspect of your mind and reinforced by the collective unconscious, incline you to buy into poverty, insecurity, illness, and unhappiness. They are the cause of all individual and social disease and neurosis. They are the very antithesis of what the ageless wisdom teaches—that the true heritage of humanity is liberation, abundance, fulfillment, and conscious immortality.

You can see then, that whatever you focus on exclusively will inevitably come about. So you must start exercising discernment regarding which images you allow to pass into your subconscious mind. Much of your initial work with the Qabalistic image of the Tree of Life is about realigning your subconscious to reflect the Divine mind of the One so that it begins to use as its point of reference an eternal and living image of the good, the beautiful, and the true.

Your subconscious mind is the most primitive mode of cognition that you have; and you share it with all incarnate life. It does not have selective logic; its assumptions are not based upon reason. Reason is an attribute of the self-conscious, or waking, mind. Your subconscious responds to the suggestions given it by your self-conscious mind without any selectivity. It acts upon the most powerful suggestions. An example of how this works is worry. Worry feeds fear into your subconscious—fear of the very thing that is worrying you. Your subconscious responds to this powerful suggestion by producing that upon which you have focused—that which you fear. When the fear manifests in your life, it reinforces the image in your subconscious and that pattern of response becomes established as a vicious spiral, set to repeat itself for as long as there is the emotional power to drive it. And you give it that power every time you reinforce it by worry. It is for this reason that worries plaguing you before sleep carry over into your subconscious the most potent of charges.

From the constructive angle, a question or problem held lightly in your mind before sleep often results in an answer received. Problems and worry are not the same thing. A problem can be dealt with creatively. Worry is a habit of the mind based on insecurity, that repeats and repeats like a needle in a groove—a groove that steadily deepens.

Another example of the unwise use of the subconscious is emotional resentment. When you replay in your imagination the emotionally charged events of the day (or of the past), when you brood on them and manipulate them in fantasy, you charge them with negative power. Many hatreds are fueled in the hours of the night; slights and mistakes are magnified out of true proportion, giving way to dark thoughts of vengeance. This is why we are advised not to let the Sun go down on our anger. This may seem a long explanation for the following exercise, the Evening Review, which is often (unwisely) regarded as a neophyte exercise. Yet much hinges upon this in later work.

One final example of the retentive nature of your subconscious mind may serve to make clear this exercise's great importance. Your subconscious retains memory of every single event in your life. At the end of each incarnation, that life-experience is reviewed by your higher self, a process traditionally known as the Halls of Osiris, or the Purgation. This can be a rather unpleasant process. In fact, the teachings of various religions on purgatory or hell states are based upon this after-death process. Eventually, what has enriched your spirit on its great journey is assimilated by your higher self and the dross—what is unworthy of eternity—is gradually dissolved into the basic matter of the various planes. This "purgation" is painful, because most of us have negative patterns so deeply entrenched in the subconscious that the light of truth consumes them like a burning fire. If, however, you have had a regular discipline of self-reflection (another name for the Evening Review), even painful experiences do not bite too deeply into your subconscious. Indeed, the Evening Review works backward, so there is more likelihood of you perceiving the underlying causes of a situation, and consequently you are less inclined to become swept along on an emotional tide.

THE EVENING REVIEW

Having composed yourself for sleep, in a gentle and relaxed state, run through the events of the day backward upon the screen of consciousness.

1. Proceed from just before you got into bed, back to the beginning of the day when you arose from bed that morning.

2. Do not get emotionally involved in the scenes, just gently observe them, as if you were watching a film.

3. If there is something that you feel ashamed of having done in the day, do not wallow in guilt and self-loathing; acknowledge the fault and make a firm intention to do better in the future.

4. If you are still awake by the end of the review, turn your mind to some idea or image of aspiration. (The tarot cards of the Hermit or Temperance are good suggestive images.)

5. Make the last impression you make upon your subconscious that night before entering the inner planes a potent suggestion of the Light.

Do not be concerned if you occasionally fall asleep during this Review. Having established the exercise as a pattern by regular practice, your deeper aspects of consciousness will continue it on inner levels. Two of the many benefits of this exercise are an increase in memory capacity and skill and a dream-state less influenced by daily events and better able to reflect the inner realities with less distortion. It has been said that a life not reflected upon is not living, merely existence.

Images of Spirit

Having established that your subconscious does think in images and retains the impression of all images introduced to it by the physical senses, we now come to one of the most potent techniques of suggestion used in the Mysteries—guided visualization. Guided visualization is the deliberate and willed imagining (image making) of symbols that are infused with spiritual meaning and force. It is a very powerful antidote to those erroneous patterns held in the personal reservoir of your subconscious. Taking primordial symbols (Divine archetypes) and building them up in your mind through the creative faculty of imagination introduces the symbols that derive from the universal mind (the Macrocosm) into your personal subconscious (the Microcosm), so that Below becomes an *accurate* reflection of Above. Once implanted there, your subconscious begins to work on and develop the symbols, making them part of your overall psychic makeup, rather like a seed once planted begins to put out roots. Realizations based on the impetus of these deep symbols are like the stems and leaves that eventually grow above the soil/surface of the unconscious. What follows is an example of a guided visualization. It will form the basis of the exercise for this chapter's practices.

GUIDED VISUALIZATION: THE CHARIOT

Ensure that you won't be disturbed, that you feel safe and secure. Perform the relaxation exercise on page 15 and establish the 4:2:4 breathing cycle (see page 16). When you feel centered, allow the images described to appear on the screen of your mind.

Be aware of the weight of your body . . . this is earth. Feel your body heat . . . this is fire. Taste the moisture in your mouth . . . this is water. Gently inhale and exhale . . . this is air. Here are the four elements of the wise held in balance in your physical body, sustaining incarnate life on the material level.

Shift your focus and be aware of the planet. The gigantic continental plates; vast floating shelves of rock, rearing to become snow-capped mountain peaks at one extreme and liquid lava at the other . . . this is earth. Be aware of the molten core of the planet, metals and rocks so hot that they flow as liquid, a nucleus of colossal power, the center by which all life on this planet is sustained . . . this is fire. Image the vast oceans that cover two-thirds of this planet's surface, the ebbing and flowing seas, the crashing waves, the glistening dew and the still mountain lakes . . . this is water. Now see the gaseous and translucent envelope that encircles the globe, transmitting solar energy in alternating tides—like planetary respiration, conducting evaporated seawater, great winds that blow over the planet from polar cap to Antarctica and about the equatorial belt, blowing as breeze or as gale across the oceans and forests . . . this is air.

Now shift again into the realm of the psyche. Swimming in the astral tides of emotional flux and flow. Is your soul presently in a state of expansion or of contraction? What situations are currently occupying your soul's attention? Past conflicts? Future apprehensions? Note them but do not engage with them.

Now move level again into the dimension of the spirit, the abode of your true self. Vast . . . immense . . . powers of cosmic proportion inhabit this realm, great alternating forces of order and chaos. This is the world of the archangels. See these shining ones . . . guardians of the courts of heaven, rank upon rank, rising up in their hosts to the four Archangels of the Presence. Now see these celestial regents: Raphael, Mikael, Gabriel, and Uriel, gathered about the footstool of the Throne of Grace., Their outstretched wings touch the edges of the universe. And you hear the unending song of the angels . . . "Holy, holy, holy"; "Holy, holy, holy"; "Holy, holy, holy."

And above them all is the Prince of the Countenances, Metatron, head of the tradition, who speaks on behalf of the Most High. He is the archangel of Kether, robed in white brilliance. Upon the forehead of this fully enlightened human and fiery spirit, shines the name of God.

Behind Metatron hangs a great curtain stretching from the highest heaven to the depths below—the *Pargod*—the tapestry of existence; each thread in this curtain is a being's life, each detail of the pattern an event in evolution.

Metatron calls you by name . . . you draw near . . . he steps aside, drawing the curtain with him . . . you step through into the presence of the Divine . . .

"A thousand years are but a moment in Thy Presence."

You hear your name called again, this time from behind . . . and you are drawn back from eternity into time and space once more. The great veil falls back in place before you . . . and Metatron speaks to you, giving a message of import to be meditated upon in future.

You descend, gently falling back from the realm of endless day . . . back through the angelic hosts . . . and into the level of the soul once more. Here, you observe the condition of your soul . . . and, having noted, you descend again into the elemental world of the manifest.

Descending through the veil of air that surrounds the planet . . . seeing the oceans and land masses . . . coming to the land, the place where you live at this time . . . descending into the building that shelters your physical body . . . you merge again with that wonderful body—the seamless garment of Adonai—integrating as one. Deeply but gently inhale and exhale . . . this is air; taste the moisture in your mouth . . . which is water; feel your body heat . . . which is fire; and feel the weight of your body, which is earth. Become aware of yourself as embodied spirit . . . and open your eyes—fully conscious—upon this level of reality.

The Exercises

To get the best results from the exercises in this book, you must perform them consistently and regularly. It is better to work regularly each day than to have an occasional spurt of enthusiasm, because it is only through regular practice that your subconscious is successfully affected and real results achieved. So I advise you to practice each day of the week, resting one day in seven. Each chapter's exercise should be practiced for thirty days. However, when undertaking real inner work of this kind, your outer level often throws up distractions to sidetrack you and divert you from the path. Sometimes, a psychological complex held in meditation is mirrored in the outer world, appearing through various situations, sometimes even crises. Obviously, at such times, you must address the outer world and regain your focus. I leave this application of self-knowledge to you so that you can acquire skill in determining what is just inertia or laziness (none of us really likes hard work) and what is a valid situation that requires your full attention. The daily practice consists of four basic parts:

- Performing the three Salutations (see page 20).

- Daily meditation (approximately fifteen minutes), using the exercises given in chapters. Ideally, each chapter's exercise should be practiced for thirty days in total, allowing for the one day's rest in seven.

- Keeping notes of the meditations and realizations in a journal or diary (see page 22).

- The Evening Review (see page 29).

A complete daily practice consists of the following steps:

1. Perform the opening Qabalistic Cross (see page 17).

2. Relax using the techniques described on page 15.

3. Establish the 4:2:4 breathing cycle (see page 16).

4. Perform the Chariot guided visualization on page 31. You may find it useful at first to record the visualization on tape, rather than distracting yourself trying to read it simultaneously or by memorizing it.

5. Relax once more.

6. Perform the closing Qabalistic Cross.

THE GLORY OF THE ELOHIM

Because the One transcends all descriptions, you can form no conception
of It, yet It is always present to those with strength to touch It.

—PLOTINUS

The entire spectrum of the teaching, philosophy, cosmology, and technical esoteric usages of the Qabalah are represented in the the Glory of the Elohim—the great symbol of the Tree of Life. (In Hebrew, this is *Etz Chaiyim,* also termed *Kavod Elohim*). Dion Fortune described this symbol as "that mighty and all-embracing glyph of the Universe and the Soul of Man."[4] In other words, the Tree symbolizes both the Macrocosm, the totality of creation, and the Microcosm, the human being. It is a symbol, not a picture. The universe does not look like the Tree of Life, nor does a human. The Tree is a mandala, a symbolic presentation of the archetypal realities that underlie all aspects of consciousness, and therefore, all existence.

The World Tree, as the Tree of Life is often called, is a motif common to many mythologies. We find it in Sumeria, Egypt, Mexico, and Scandinavia. This World Tree represents the *axis mundi,* the immovable center around which all circles, upon which all is dependent. It symbolizes the possibility of ascent from the lower to the higher levels, of refuge under its branches, and of ongoing sustenance from its fruit. At a deep level, there is hidden the knowledge of the sharing of breath: A tree breathes in carbon dioxide and exhales oxygen, while a human inhales oxygen and breathes out carbon dioxide. Trees are a universal symbol of life, and their cultivation is an indication of abundance. The Arabic from which our word "paradise" comes means "a garden of trees"; the Divine world of Atziluth is sometimes referred to as the Holy Orchard.

The Qabalistic Tree of Life symbolizes all that is, both as the One-in-All and as the Many-in-One. It is a pictorial representation of the whole to all of its parts, and of their interrelatedness within the whole. It is a hieroglyph (a sacred sign) of relationship, of oneness, of unity. This is why so many of the sacrificial gods that hang upon the Tree—Osiris, Jesus, Baldur, Dionysus—represent the way of return to a state of at-one-ment with the whole.

The Tree of Life

Figure 1 (see page 39) shows the classical form of the Tree of Life (sometimes called the Cordovero Tree).

The Tree has many forms, however, because the symbol, like the Qabalistic tradition itself, has evolved over time. The ten spheres of the diagram are collectively called, in Hebrew, the *sephiroth* (pronounced: sefirot). The singular noun is *sephira* (pronounced: sefira). The word has several meanings, among them, "precious vessels" and "sapphires" (hence this book's title). The Western tree is identical to the Asian "net of jewels," for they both come from the Primordial Teaching. The lines

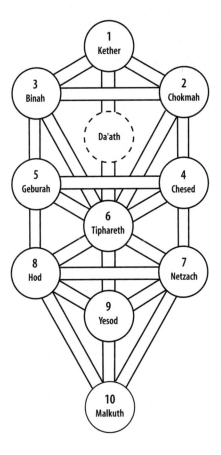

Figure 1. The Tree of Life.

connecting the sephiroth are called the paths. The original Hebrew term for these paths is translated as "canals," from the idea of the sephiroth as reservoirs of grace. Together, these sephiroth and the connecting pathways constitute the thirty-two Paths of Wisdom. This may seem confusing, but it becomes clear when you realize that the sephiroth are pathways too.

39

Many find the Hebrew terminology of the Qabalah daunting; the lazy find it off-putting. But you don't have to be able to speak or read Hebrew to practice the Qabalah successfully. Like any science, Qabalah has its own jargon—specialized terms that communicate associated ideas to those familiar with the terms. It is quite possible for two Qabalists with no common language to have a fruitful exchange by using the diagram of the Tree of Life and the twenty-two tarot keys of the Major Arcana. This jargon of the Qabalah becomes familiar through use.

Hebrew is a living tongue, unlike Latin, Classical Greek, or ancient Egyptian. Indeed, millions of people speak and pray in it everyday. So there is no reason why students of the Qabalah should not pronounce it correctly. In fact, not to do so is to weaken its invocatory powers. There are too many cases of Western Mystery students (and sometimes teachers) approaching Rabbinic Qabalists intent on a meaningful exchange, and finding that they cannot be understood at all. So throughout this book, where Hebrew is used, I will spell it as it is usually transliterated into English (so that you don't become confused when reading other books on the subject), but I will always endeavor to give the correct pronunciation. Hebrew has two dialects: Ashkenazi from Eastern Europe, and Sephardi from North Africa and the Middle East. Sephardi is the dialect used in the Western esoteric tradition. The term *Sephardi* means "Spanish" and refers to the descendants of the Jews expelled from Spain by Isabella and Ferdinand. Most of the Jews from Spain settled in parts of the Ottoman Empire, which included North Africa; some went to Palestine (as it was then) and founded several Qabalistic communities, the most famous being Safed near the Sea of Galilee. The form of Qabalah practiced by Sephardic Jews was that of the Toledo tradition, whose philosophy is closest to that of the Alchemical Qabalah.

Table 1. The Ten Lights of Emanation on the Tree of Life

SEPHIRA	PRONUNCIATION	TRANSLATION
1-Kether	Keter	Crown
2-Chokmah	Hokma	Wisdom
3-Binah	Bina	Understanding
4-Chesed	Hesed	Mercy
5-Geburah	Gevura	Strength
6-Tiphareth	Tifaret	Beauty
7-Netzach	Nezak	Victory
8-Hod	Hod	Splendor
9-Yesod	Yesud	Foundation
10-Malkuth	Malkut	Kingdom

We'll begin our analysis of the Tree with the ten lights of emanation, the sephiroth (see figure 1, page 39). Table 1 gives their number, name, pronunciation, and translation, beginning with the topmost sphere and proceeding downward.

The name of the Withdrawn Sephira, Da'ath, is pronounced "Da'at." It is called the "withdrawn" or the "non-sephira" because Da'ath always belongs to the world *preceding* that depicted by the Tree.

The sephiroth are linked by paths that form triangles and triads as they cross and meet each other. Each individual path joins two sephiroth, and the energies of the connected spheres flow through the path, so that each path partakes of the qualities of the sephiroth it unites.

There are two major ways in which the sephiroth of the Tree are grouped: pillars and countenances. Seen vertically, the spheres of the

Tree consist of three columns. These columns are called the pillars. From right to left:

- The column of Chokmah, Chesed, and Netzach is the Pillar of Force.
- The column of Kether, Tiphareth, Yesod, and Malkuth is the Middle Pillar, called the Pillar of Consciousness when looking upward and the Pillar of Grace when looking downward.
- The column of Binah, Geburah, and Hod is the Pillar of Form.

The Tree contains two countenances: the Greater Countenance, formed by Kether, Chokmah, Binah, and Tiphareth (with Da'ath in the center), and the Lesser Countenance, formed by Tiphareth, Netzach, Hod, and Malkuth (with Yesod in the center). Tiphareth is placed in both countenances, as the bottom of the Greater and the top of the Lesser. In this lies an important key, for, in Tiphareth, face can gaze upon face.

If you follow the numbers given in table 1, you see that the numerical sequence is horizontal when reading from right to left, diagonal when reading from left to right, and vertical for the final two spheres, 9 and 10. This sequence is called the Lightning Flash (also known as the Fiery Sword). It is an esoteric formula used often in the practical Qabalah. One of the teachings it shows us is that perception of a higher plane is usually achieved through the form aspect of that plane. Any force being imparted from a higher to a lower plane appears on the inferior plane as a form. In a certain sense, the white Pillar of Force, as the initiating principle, represents the past, while the black Pillar of Form, as the principle of embodiment, represents the future. The gold Middle Pillar, the Pillar of Grace, synthesizes and holds the side pillars in harmonious balance. It represents the Holy Now, the ever-present moment.

The Lightning Flash is the sequence by which the sephiroth emanate one from another. To the ancients who constructed the Qabalah, a flash of lightning was the brightest and fastest phenomenon to be seen in the natural world. Both of these root concepts of speed and brilliance are important—they combine to suggest "in the twinkling of a Divine eye." The emanation of the sephiroth is not spatial or temporal; they existed even before time and space. Neither are the sephiroth or the paths actually cosmic spheres and lines appearing somewhere in the manifested universe. They are states of consciousness and they pervade all that is.

The sequence of the Lightning Flash from Kether descending to Malkuth is the way of involution—the One Life-Power descending, plane by plane, and veiling itself in denser vibratory states. The sequence of the Lightning Flash from Malkuth ascending to Kether is the way of evolution—termed the Path of Return, culminating in union with the Indivisible One. In 12th-century Spain, it was said that the Tree of Life was like "a ladder into Heaven"; and so it is. Once you have established the Tree within your subtle bodies and aura by meditation, you can use its Lightning Flash to ascend into the worlds on high. Most important, you can also use it to return safely into fully embodied consciousness. Details of this practice will be taught later.

The Middle Pillar

The Middle Pillar, the Pillar of Consciousness or the Pillar of Grace, is the tallest of the three pillars on the Tree. It spans the level of pure divinity right down through the planes of spirit and psyche, to stand in the plane of full materiality. It is thus the harmonious balancing of the energies of the force and form. It is the Middle Way taught by the Lord Gautama Buddha, and practiced by all sane occultists and mystics. Table 2 gives the Divine names attributed to the sephiroth of the Middle Pillar.

Table 2. The Divine Names of the Middle Pillar Sephiroth

SEPHIRA	HEBREW NAME	TRANSLATION
Kether	Eheieh	I am
Da'ath	Yaveh-Elohim	The One Reality creates
Tiphareth	Yaveh-Eloah-ve-Da'ath	The One Reality knows all and accomplishes all
Yesod	Shaddai-El-Chai	Living Almighty One
Malkuth	Adonai-ha-Aretz	Ruler of the Earth

In the Macrocosm—(the universe), Kether is the Primal Will-to-Good that is the crown of creation. The invisible sephira Da'ath leads to other dimensions and worlds. Tiphareth, which is the heart of the Tree, is the Solar Logos, the great being whose vehicle/body is the star of our own solar system. Yesod is the astral plane and the treasure house of souls. Malkuth is the kingdom of the manifested universe, the beautiful yet transitory blossom on the Tree of Life.

In the Microcosm (the individual human), Kether is the self-of-the-self, *Yechidah*, the unique and indivisible, the Divine spark. Da'ath is the window or mirror through which you see the outer physical world and your own inner kingdom. Tiphareth is the seat of your higher self, the Holy Guardian Angel that is your real self. This is your spirit and your awareness of being aware; the vehicle you use in this realm is your mental body. The self in Tiphareth is called *ruach* in Hebrew, which is, in fact, a metathesis of the name of the Egyptian god, Horus. Yesod is the level of your astral and etheric bodies. It is also the seat of the vital soul, sometimes called the animal soul (*nephesh* in Hebrew). It is the realm of your psyche, your individual soul that constitutes your incarnate personality, often termed the lower self to distinguish it from the higher self that is the true "I." Malkuth is your physical body in its totality (some 30 trillion cells), the seamless garment of Adonai, the vehicle you use to experience the physical realm directly. This microcosmic Middle Pillar shows diagrammatically that your total selfhood dwells simultaneously in many dimensions.

Transcendence

A high Tibetan lama, when speaking on the theme of spiritual work, emphasized that religion and spirituality are distinct from one another. The metaphor he used was that religion was like a boat used for crossing a broad river. Having successfully crossed the river, however, the boat becomes a weighty encumbrance. It's hard to travel beyond the river with a boat on your back!

The same can be said of Qabalah. You may think this an obvious point, but observation shows that many students of Qabalah think of it as a mystical adjunct to their chosen or inherited religion. Sadly, we see a form of "Yetziratic fundamentalism" in which students from different streams of Qabalah regard those of other streams as in error. Rabbinic and orthodox Qabalists condemn "Goy Qabalists" (and women Qabalists); Christian Qabalists and Rosicrucians look down on non-Christian Qabalists; and so it goes on. And none of this takes into account the bickering that sadly occurs between schools who belong to the *same* stream of Qabalah. Can we call this spiritual work—each presuming that they own something that actually belongs to the Divine? For Qabalah is imparted from Above and is ultimately bestowed by God.

Religion is a garment worn by truth, and few people wear the same clothes all the time. The purpose of religion is to enable people to control the nefesh and to begin to develop a truly human soul. Its purpose is to civilize and refine both individuals and societies. But religion is not, and never has been, the end result. As one teacher said: "Do not confuse the scaffolding with the finished Temple." Humanity is still in process; it is still evolving. In a sense, we are the unripe green apples on the Tree of Life.

In his esoteric novel, *The Anointed*, Z'ev ben Shimon Halevi describes an authentic Qabalistic group composed of Jews, Christians, and Moslems—all the Children of the Book—united by the Work. The group's leader, Don Immauel (a Jew), becomes the Messiah of the time; he is succeeded in that august role by Hakim, a Moslem. There is no religious rivalry in this group, no particular religion held up as "the one" to make other religionists feel as if they are second-class or in error. This group reflects, in Assiah, the Briatic Great Holy Council, which is composed of the sages from all cultures, religions, and times who have realized the unity of God, which transcends all man-made divisions.

The Chinese have a saying: One who has mastered a tradition can then eat of the fruit of other traditions. A realized spiritual practitioner can worship with others in any setting because they have learned to be conscious of the Divine in all places and in all beings. The unity, the oneness, is not realized by myopic or blinkered vision. The Divine impulse behind any new religion is to liberate, but within a few generations, it hardens. Unless it is renewed by fresh revelation, it will soon fossilize. Theology, that tool of agnostics, is often nothing more than a hair-splitting indulgence of Hod.

BUILDING THE MIDDLE PILLAR

To begin, perform the opening Qabalistic Cross (see page 17), then perform the relaxation exercise on page 15. Establish the 4:2:4 breath cycle as described on page 16). For the first two weeks you use this exercise, follow these steps:

1. Imagine a sphere of dazzling white brilliance above your head.

2. With an exhalation of breath, see a beam of white light descend and form another sphere of white light in the area of your throat.

3. Exhale again and see a beam descend from the second sphere to establish a third sphere of light in your chest region.

4. Continue the same process to build a fourth sphere in your genital region, then, finally, a fourth encompassing the ankles and feet.

5. Use your imagination to build the intensity of the spheres. Allow their radiance to permeate you (see figure 2, page 48).

For the rest of the meditation period, bathe in the influence of these spheres of Divine light. To end the exercise, perform the closing Qabalistic Cross and write an entry in your journal.

For the second two weeks, begin as described above, performing the opening Qabalistic Cross and the relaxation exercise, then establish the 4:2:4 breath cycle. Now build the middle spheres as before, but visualize them in their appropriate colors as described on page 49 (see also figure 3, page 50).

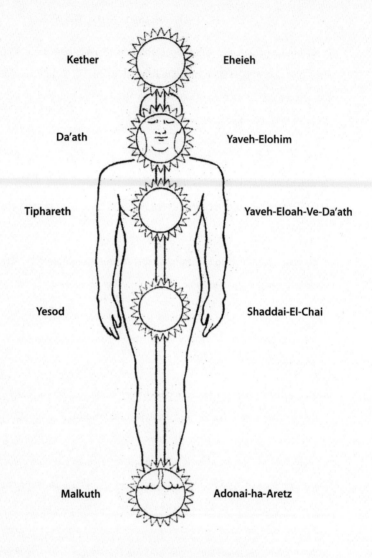

Kether		Eheieh
Da'ath		Yaveh-Elohim
Tiphareth		Yaveh-Eloah-Ve-Da'ath
Yesod		Shaddai-El-Chai
Malkuth		Adonai-ha-Aretz

Figure 2. Building the Middle Pillar.

1. Focus on Kether above your head, and intone *EHEIEH.*

2. Focus on your throat center and intone *YAHVEH-ELOHIM.* See the sphere become pale gray in color.

3. At your chest center, intone *YAHVEH-ELOAH-VE-DA'ATH* and see the sphere become golden-yellow in color.

4. At your genital center, intone *SHADDAI-EL-CHAI* and see the sphere become violet in hue.

5. At your feet center, intone *ADONAI-HA-ARETZ* and see the sphere become dark indigo-blue in color.

    For the remainder of the meditation period, rest in the vitalizing power of the Divine lights of emanation. To end the exercise, perform the closing Qabalistic Cross and write an entry in your journal.

Figure 3 diagrams the above exercise with circles depicting the colors of the spheres of light. Color in the blank circles and paths in figure 4 (see page 51) according to the directions given in the exercise and in figure 3. Felt-tip pens or acrylic paints work well. Then color all the remaining space, including that between the paths, black. Write the names of the sephiroth (Kether, etc.) on the spheres. Hang it over the altar in your sacred space, so that you are seated opposite it during your future meditation sessions.

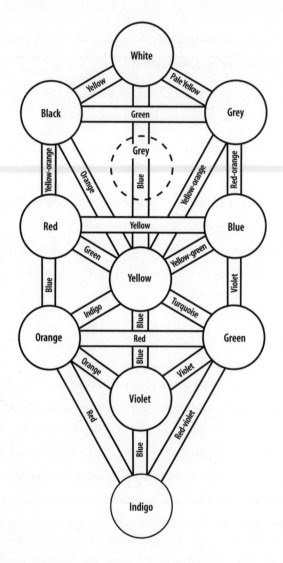

Figure 3. Colors of the Spheres and Paths in the Tree of Life.

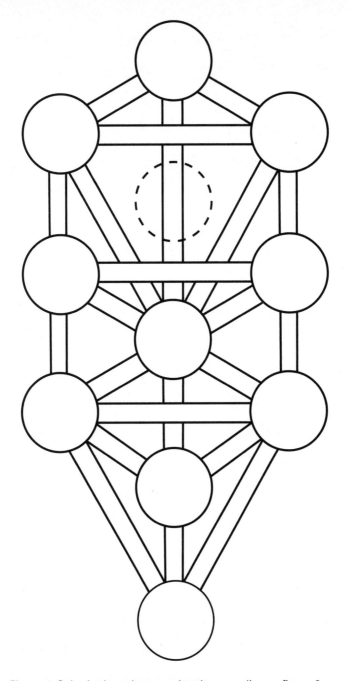

Figure 4. Color in the spheres and paths according to figure 3.

THE CROWN
AND THE KINGDOM

As Above so Below, but after a different manner.

—Emerald Tablet of Hermes Trismegistos

The quotation above implies that the One Power that creates and sustains the outer universe (the kingdom of Malkuth) is the same power that enables you to re-create your inner kingdom. Your outer life, all the factors and circumstances that constitute your personal environment, are the direct result of this One Power working through you. If there is any want, dis-ease, or poverty in your life, this is not due to some inadequacy on the part of the One Power. It is due to your inability to express that power clearly and without distortion. The more transparent you are to the Divine—the One Power—the more abundantly it flows through you, perfecting, enriching, and transforming all aspects of your life.

Because your outer life is the manifestation of your interior state, to bring about change in your circumstances, you must make subtle alterations within your inner kingdom. This simple, yet profound, fact is the basis of all magic. As the Native American medicine people say: Dream the right dreams, then dance the dreams awake.

The One Reality

On some representations of the Tree of Life, three semicircles are drawn above Kether. These are the Three Veils. They are also called the Veils of Negative Existence, to intimate that the order of existence they represent totally transcends any criteria by which we measure life. The veils are incomprehensible, beyond anything that the brain-consciousness of current incarnate humanity can realize. They represent absolute existence, as distinct from relative existence. They are descriptions of the Absolute, of the primordial ground of being. They are, in Hebrew, *Ain* ("nothing," or "No-thing"), *Ain-Soph* ("the Infinite"), and *Ain-Soph-Aur* ("the Limitless Light"). They may be envisaged as the Northern Lights, the *Aurora Borealis*, shimmering in the dark void beyond the white brilliance of Kether.

The Absolute—the transcendent—is termed "No-thing" because there is no thing to which it may be likened or compared. It is the ineffable glory before which even the angels veil their faces, for to all manifest creatures, the Limitless Light of the Absolute appears as the thrice-radiant darkness. For this reason, the Divine names of the sephiroth are written in black ink, to represent the black fire (the veiled light) of Ain. For the same reason, the eyes are closed in meditation and covered in prayer; for in deepest meditation or at the height of mystical prayer, we return to the void, to the No-thing of the Absolute. This profound state of consciousness is described in the texts of the ageless wisdom as *being* with God. Like the angels, we veil our faces and are alone with the Alone (who is the All-One). Jacob Boehme put it well when he wrote:

If thou canst, my son, for a while but cease from all thy thinking
and willing, then thou shalt hear the unspeakable words of God
. . . When thou art quiet and silent, then art thou as God was
before nature and creature; thou art that which God then was;
thou art that of which he made thy nature and creature: Then
thou hearest and seest even with that wherewith God himself
saw and heard in thee, before ever thine own willing or thine
own seeing began.[5]

Ain is also represented by the black background of the colored Tree of
Life diagram (see page 51). This Tree, representing manifestation, is set
within the infinity of the No-thing, set within the zero. Ain, the One
Reality, is that which is truly eternal. It is the Great Initiator, who is the
rootless root of all being, the causeless cause of all that is. In that, we live,
and move, and have our being.

Looking at the Tree, we see that the thrice-radiant darkness of Ain
not only forms the backdrop of the Tree, but is also found between each
sephira and each path. It permeates all existence. In the Western
Mysteries, one of the titles of the Absolute is The Great One of the Night
of Time, represented in the sacred tarot by Key XXI, the World. There is
much in this that will bear fruit if meditated upon.

Everything, visible and invisible, on all levels of existence, is formed
of the radiant energy originating in the Absolute that enters into manifestation through the hollow crown of Kether. There are various terms in
occultism for this radiant energy, and you should familiarize yourself
with them: the One Thing, the Limitless Light, L.V.X., the One Force, the
Life-power, and the Primal Will.

Each and every being is essentially a pattern of this energy expressing
the livingness of the One. And the Eternal One is the inmost center of
each of its expressions, whether that individual expression be as an

archangel or an ant, a star or an atom. The Absolute is the dweller in the temple of every human personality. Everything you have ever seen in your life is God—and none other.

It is for this reason that all rituals of the Mysteries of Light commence with the invocation of the One in Kether, thereby drawing unmanifest energy through Kether into manifestation so that your work enhances and adorns creation as you cocreate with God. In this way, you do not rob energy from any manifest source—as does the sorcerer or dabbler—which would cause imbalances within the universe.

The Master Pattern

The Absolute (pure consciousness) is the Great Mystery. We will be better occupied, at this stage, if we consider the Absolute in manifestation. So we start our study with that which we can begin to comprehend— the will, which is consciousness—in action. This is symbolized by the Tree of Life, since the Tree is the master pattern upon the trestle-board of the Grand Architect of the Universe, the template of existence. By studying the relationships that the Tree symbolizes, you learn of the potencies and attributes of the One Thing, and, since you are its offspring, of yourself as well. You study the Eternal through its manifestations. Western monasticism calls this practice "reading from *Liber-Mundi*, the Book of the World." This is also what the alchemists meant by studying the Book of Nature. By the penetrative observation of the Microcosm, you receive intimations of the Macrocosm. Through your seeking to know God—made manifest in nature, you receive gradual realizations that increase in frequency and duration, and culminate in a living and continuous experience of the transcendent. For, although the Absolute *is* transcendent, it is nearer than hands and feet, nearer than breath. It is not remote, but eternally present, everywhere—in the eternal now.

What has all this to do with magic? How do these metaphysical realities connect to occult science? Few people truly comprehend the Magic of Light; indeed, those who say they know often prove to be the most ignorant.

The universe—all relative existence—is *continually* being created. It is by the radiant energy—proceeding from the Absolute, and mediated by the Hierarchy to the incarnate servants of God—that the worlds are nourished and sustained.

The practice of transcendental magic (*Theurgy*) is based upon the knowledge that whatever the objective, that objective *already exists* as a reality in the upper worlds. It simply has not yet manifested. A true mage does not seek to impose personal will onto people or circumstances. Rather, the mage rises in consciousness and receives from Above the patterns that are willed. Then, by allowing the Divine Will to be clothed in his or her consciousness—in an act of transparent cocreation through the mage's instrumentality—what was formally interior becomes manifested in form or substance. All authentic advancements in civilization or evolution are really unveilings of the Infinite One.

There is an aphorism in yoga that the *enlightened* man is more powerful than the gods themselves, because his slightest wish becomes a universal imperative. Therefore, Theurgy is an act of submission to, and cooperation with, the omnipotence of the Divine. It is the fulfillment of what Jesus taught in his prayer: "Thy will be done on earth *as it is* in heaven." Theurgy is the "will to beauty" (Tiphareth), because it beautifies relative existence in accordance with the will of the One. Transcendental magic is the ongoing work of manifesting heaven on Earth.

To the degree that you open yourself to the radiant energy of the One, your life and circumstances will be transformed. For the crown to rule the kingdom, you must align your personal will with the will expressed by the crown; then will the abundance of the One flower in your life. This crown is Kether, and none other.

It is important that you not become too fixated upon the vertical aspect of the Tree of Life. Occult texts often use terms like "rising on the planes," "ascension," or "raising consciousness." Such terms can incline you to think that the sephiroth are somehow above you, that you are traveling in an upward direction. Whereas, when we speak of "ascending" the Tree, we could equally say "going behind" or "going within," meaning to go behind outer appearances, or to go within your being. The One is the Inmost as well as the Most High. On the Tree, Kether represents this Divine self, which is your deepest identity at your inmost center. This is why the Divine name of Kether is *Eheieh*, which means "I am." It signifies pure existence; it is what we mean when we say "I"; it is our sense of enduring selfhood. Phonetically, Eheieh sounds like breath being exhaled and, in your meditation techniques, you link up your breath with the willed direction of the radiant energy.

Kether is the lens that focuses the radiant energy from the Absolute into creation. This radiant energy, this light, is the sole substance of everything. This is not just a piece of metaphysics; it is a scientific fact. Scientists in our time have discovered what the Mysteries have taught for millennia—that everything is composed of energy. This energy is indestructible and pervades everything. It is electromagnetic by nature. At an atomic level, electrons whirl about their nucleus in the same way that planets orbit their suns (as Above, so Below . . .); the nucleus of each atom is a center of radiant light. This radiant light is diffused throughout space—there is nowhere that it is not. Every single thing that you see, touch, taste, smell, or hear is an adaptation of this single radiant energy. So we have both the report of those-who-know, and that of modern physicists, both of which state (using different terminology) that the omnipresence of the One is a fact.

In the Qabalah, this radiant life-force is called *chaiah*, and is attributed to Chokmah, the second sphere of the Tree of Life, the sphere of the zodiac, the sphere of the stars. Stars are the first condensation of this Limitless Light. The omnipresence of the One is called *Neschamah*, the Divine soul, and is attributed to Binah. Binah is the Great Manifest, the womb of creation in which all things are grown. But, the seed that impregnates the forms of Binah is the eternal radiant energy flowing from Chokmah, the All-Father. However, the origin of both Chokmah and Binah lies in Kether, the crown. Everything you learn about any of the sephiroth—indeed anything you learn anywhere—has its root, its source, in Kether. As mentioned before, this is why all rituals of the Magic of Light begin with the invocation of Kether. It aligns you with the creative source; it plugs you into the cosmic generator. When you perform the Qabalistic Cross, it is Kether that is first visualized as a diadem of light over your head. And in the Middle Pillar formula (see page 47), the radiant energy (white brilliance) is brought down through Kether and earthed in the kingdom of Malkuth. For there is an important truth regarding the radiant energy that science has not yet discovered—a truth that practitioners of the Mysteries exploit. The radiant energy is *mental* in origin, and can be directed by mind.

Because the radiant energy is not apparent to your physical senses (although you see the forms it has built everywhere), it is called the "Hidden Light" (*Aur Mopla* in Hebrew), and also the "Inner Light" (*Aur Penimi* in Hebrew), because it is the center of every human being. Both of these terms are also titles of Kether. The Hidden Light is the originator and the sole support of all existence; it pervades and fills all things. But this Hidden Light is not something *other* than yourself, something apart from you. Your deepest nature is identical with it—not *was* in some distant past, or *will be* at the end of evolutionary time, but *now*. You are not becoming like God; you are already God in the unveiling. The purpose of the Mysteries, of all true occultism, is to enable you to come to a firsthand knowledge of your glorious heritage, your birthright. You are an eternal being of light. With inner vision, you can perceive yourself and your world, awash in a boundless ocean of splendor, streaming from the stars, and wearing an infinite variety of forms. You can see your body as it really is: as some 30 trillion points of diamond brilliance that comprise each form, each a true chalice of light.

Your eternal and Divine self, is called *Yechidah* ("the unique, the indivisible") and is attributed to Kether. This is the crown you put on to rule your inner kingdom. *Gnothi Seauton* ("Know Thyself"), which was written over the Greek Mystery temples really meant to know *the* self. Knowledge—not faith or intellectual assent—knowledge of the real self is the purpose of the Mysteries. And all true initiations and grades in the Mysteries are steps in the unfolding of that knowledge in ever-greater degree.

It may seem to some that the foregoing is rather abstract for an early chapter on Qabalah. But it seems important to me that, before setting out upon a journey, you have some idea about the destination. It gives you a point by which you can read your compass. This will save you from the many pitfalls and dangers that often beset those who work with occult forces. Before we leave this theme for the time being, use the following quotation as a subject for reflection. It is from an alchemical treatise entitled *The Salt of Nature Regenerated*, written by the sage Alipili:

He that hath knowledge of the Microcosm cannot long be ignorant of the Macrocosm. This is that which the Egyptian industrious searchers of Nature so often said, and loudly proclaimed . . . that everyone should Know Himself.

. . . But I admonish thee, whosoever thou art, that desirest to dive into the inmost parts of Nature, if that which thou seekest thou find not within thee, thou wilt never find it without thee . If thou knowest not the excellency of thine own house, why dost thou seek and search after the excellency of other things? The universal Orb of the World contains not so many great mysteries and excellencies as a little Man, formed by God in His own image. And he who desirest the primacy among the students of Nature will nowhere find a greater or better field of study than himself.

Therefore will I follow the example of the Wise, and speak from my whole heart, and from certain true experiences proved by me, and in the words of the Egyptians, and with a loud voice, do now proclaim: "Oh Man, Know Thyself, in Thee is hidden the **Treasure of all Treasures.**[6]

The Work of the Moon

How does this relate to the meditation practice we have been performing? In the last chapter, you began your work on the Tree of Life with the Middle Pillar Exercise (see page 47). You began by bringing the radiant energy through you and thereby invigorating your center. The radiance entered into your "sphere of sensation" and nourished and empowered it. This sphere of sensation is your totality. Sitting where you are, reading these words, you are an immortal and eternal being who is wearing a series of vestures, bodies, or sheaths—a Divine spark wearing a mental, astral, etheric, and physical body. Each of these vehicles or bodies coexist within each other; they are not separate and apart, but, like Russian matrushka dolls, interpenetrate one another. This is most clearly seen when viewing a person's aura; the bands of color radiating outward show how spiritual, mental, astral, and etheric bodies are present as one inclusive sphere.

In the Middle Pillar Exercise, cosmic energy is brought in and channeled through all of your bodies, and on into the planet. The incoming energy stimulates the various bodies in its passage through them. Each body is made dynamic, and in turn, passes the current into the next body. This is not something you must do yourself; it happens quite naturally. If you attend a concert, the music (which originated as inspiration on the mental plane) may affect your astral body (your emotional response to the music) and may go on to affect your physical body: goose bumps, a smile, or perhaps tears.

It is your etheric body that is the principal focus in the Middle Pillar Exercise, and for the other exercises built upon its foundation. The etheric level is the interface between the lower astral and the physical. (This is also the level of the nature spirits and the elemental beings: gnomes, undines, sylphs, and salamanders.) The etheric aura is the most easily seen; it usually appears as a thin band of blue-white light extending from the physical body, about two to five inches in width. It is the etheric body that channels the radiant energy into the physical. This takes place primarily during sleep, and is the reason for your need to sleep. It is a strain for the physical vehicle to be indwelt by human self-consciousness, which is, in fact, an intense and sophisticated concentration of consciousness. To hold such a unit of consciousness in embodiment requires much energy. Some of the required energy is drawn from food, air, and liquid. But the greater amount is replenished in sleep. You can live longer without food than without sleep. Your etheric body draws radiant energy directly from the stars and suns, from the great ocean of living power that fills the universe. All self-conscious beings require sleep to revitalize their earthly bodies; fish, animals, and birds all require rest so that the etheric can nourish the physical. On this planet, humans alone have the ability to draw upon the infinite reservoir of energy *at will*. This is what we are practicing in the exercises of this book.

In ritual magic, any power invoked has to pass through the vehicles of those working the rite. But to bring power right through into earth, it must pass through the etheric body and on through the physical. If this does not occur, the power becomes aborted; it remains on the astral, finding no opening into the planes below, and will then either dissipate or return to its own realm. This is why so many attempts at ritual work by untrained people produce sporadic, hit-and-miss results. Many people have astral vision and flexibility, but few indeed have learned how to bring the power through and so become true mages. The Middle Pillar Exercise is the first step and the basis of etheric training, known in the old texts as the Work of the Moon.

The Rainbow Scale

In the last chapter, I suggested that you draw and color a diagram of the Tree of Life (see figure 4, page 51). It is surprising the number of so-called students of Qabalah and occultism who have never drawn or colored such a diagram. These "armchair occultists" (theorists and academics) regard such practices as childish, as too simple for their advanced attention. Why do I suggest that you learn to draw and to color your own copies of the sacred mandala of the West? This is not some child's coloring exercise. When you color your own diagram, it becomes inseparably linked to you. The attention you give it impresses the symbol of the Tree upon your brain cells and builds the details into your consciousness. Making the Tree of Life a part of yourself is one of the most practical secrets of all occultism. Among other things, it connects you to the group-soul and the group-mind of the Qabalah that is comprised of all the Great Ones and their students throughout history who have achieved their liberation through the use of the Tree of Life. When the Tree has been inscribed on your subconscious by the atten-

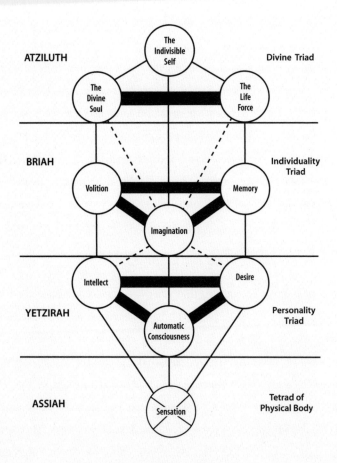

Figure 5. The Four Worlds.

tive act of drawing or coloring, the telepathic power of your subconscious (which we all possess) brings you into rapport with those who have used the Tree as a ladder to the Divine. A diagram of the Tree that you have made and colored is a truly potent spiritual tool. Its power for suggestion is far greater than that which can be obtained from any copy purchased in a shop or made by another. This why you should place the Tree of Life you made in the space where you perform your daily meditations.

During the second two weeks of the Middle Pillar Exercise (see page 49), you visualized the sephiroth of the Middle Pillar in color. What you perceived as color is the result of different frequencies of light—different rates of vibration being received by your eyes. So color is used to identify the influences of the various sephiroth manifesting in creation. The science of color is employed in magic for many purposes. Essentially, however, you use color to select the power you intend to use. By using the appropriate color, you attune your subjective consciousness to the vibration rate of the objective power. When the link is so made, your consciousness becomes a channel through which the cosmic power can flow.

It will now be obvious that white brilliance is assigned to Kether because the crown is the source of everything in manifestation. White contains all the colors, as Kether contains the potential of all that is. The colors used for the Middle Pillar Exercise are drawn from what is called the Queen scale or the rainbow colors. This is the set of colors attributed to the Tree of Life in Briah. Briah is one of the Four Worlds of the Qabalah: *Atziluth* (the archetypal world of emanation), *Briah* (the archangelic world of creation), *Yetzirah* (the angelic world of astral formation), and *Assiah* (the material, physical universe). Figure 5 depicts these worlds on the Tree (see page 64).

Table 3. Attributions of the Tree of Life

SEPHIRA	COLOR	ARCHANGEL
Kether	white brilliance	Metatron
Chokmah	gray	Ratziel
Binah	black/indigo	Tzaphkiel
Da'ath	lavender	Uriel
Chesed	blue	Tzadkiel
Geburah	red	Khamael
Tiphareth	yellow	Michael
Netzach	green	Haniel
Hod	orange	Raphael
Yesod	violet	Gabriel
Malkuth	citrine, olive, russet & black	Sandalphon

In subjective work, it is the color scale of Briah that is used. This is because Briah, the world of creation, is the realm of the spirit—the higher self—and much of your early work is spent in consciously drawing the influence of your higher self through to transmute your personality.

By working with the Tree in Briah, you bypass, to a certain extent, those astral forms in Yetzirah that are distortions of spiritual realities. The astral level (Yetzirah) is as much a mixture of good and evil as is the physical level (Assiah). By working with the spiritual energies of Briah, which are also those superconscious powers of your own higher self, you bring that influence through the astral level. Here, the influence of spirit begins to make subtle adjustments and corrections to the distorted astral images that we all have in our psyches. The spiritual power of Briah, containing as it does the Divine ideals, imprints and establishes new patterns within your subconscious that clearly mirror, without distortion, the higher realities. This then assists your physical life and environment to become truer reflections in earth (Assiah) of the Primal Will-to-Good. Detailed teachings regarding the Four Worlds will be part of a later chapter. Our principal focus at this stage is to learn to use the Tree of Life as a channel for the life-power.

Table 3 (page 66) gives a list of the attributions of the Tree in the world of Briah, showing each sephira's name, its color, and the archangel who is its spiritual focus.

For preliminary work, the sphere of Malkuth is visualized either as totally indigo/black or citrine (a yellow-green). In later stages, this sephira is visualized in all four colors. The gray of Chokmah actually appears to clairvoyant sight as an opalescent gray, shot through with flashes of rainbow tints—for in Chokmah, the white brilliance of Kether is prismatically broken up. The indigo of Binah is blue-violet.

Sacred Space

Meditation works with powerful forces, forces that will bring about transformation and transmutation on all levels. In fact, when you enter into a state of meditation, you are participating in the same activity by which the One creates and sustains all that is. The only difference is in *degree*, not in *type*. Your meditation is subjective; the meditation of the Absolute is cosmic. But both are, in essence, acts of self-reflection.

Whenever possible, you should do your regular meditation in the same place. This practice builds up an atmosphere that is conducive to interior work, and also assists you during periodic "dry spells." When you imagine the sephiroth in their colors, which are aspects of the radiant energy, you suffuse your meditation area with light from Above. By speaking the Divine names, which are also names of power, you key your meditation space in to those energies and it begins to absorb and radiate them in turn.

To speak a Divine name correctly means to speak it with consciousness. If you hear someone call out your name, it attracts your attention and you become aware of the caller. When speaking the holy names of God, you must be aware of whose name you are speaking, and whose attention you have alerted. This is why there is a commandment against speaking the Divine names in vain, without reverent attention.

A ritual altar is a throne of light, a seat prepared for the Eternal as the guest of honor. By setting up an altar in your meditation space, you say to the Divine, "Come and sit with me. Take up your abode with me. Accept this place as your own." An altar is also a space made for your inner world to manifest, a stage for the interior archetypes to appear upon.

In the ceremonial workings of the Western Mystery Tradition, the altar in the temple is the sacred axis around which the energies revolve. Everything is focused on the altar as the visible symbol of the immanence. The altar is the gateway of spirit. It is upon the altar of sacrifice that an initiate's dedication is made, for all time.

By physically creating an altar, you exteriorize the true altar that is within the sanctuary of your heart. To make such an altar is simple. What is essential is that every act connected with establishing an altar be done with deep intention. You may use a small table, a mantelpiece, a desk, or a chest of drawers. The surface should be covered with a clean white cloth—a large handkerchief or square scarf can be used—but it must be new, having been used for no other purpose. The white cloth signifies the purity of your intention.

At the center of the altar, place a lamp or a single candle. If you use a lamp, it should be of red glass and contain a night-light. If you use a candle, it should be white. Light this lamp or candle before each meditation session, and extinguish it afterward. The burning flame is the Light of the World, which the darkness cannot overcome. It is an outward symbol of the Hidden Light within you—child of the Most High.

It is a good practice, when lighting the lamp, to imagine the light coming from your heart center to ignite the wick. When extinguishing the lamp, visualize the light returning into the shrine of your heart.

You may also place upon the altar a picture or image of any Great One—a master, saint, or god-form—who is for you an example of the Eternal. On the wall over the altar, place the Tree of Life diagram that you colored. Place the chair you use for meditation facing the altar. It is also good practice to burn some incense while meditating. Incense has a powerful effect upon your midbrain and your subconscious mind. A good-quality frankincense is ideal for meditation work.

THE FOUR WORLDS EXERCISE

Perform the opening Qabalistic Cross (see page 17), then perform the relaxation exercise on page 15. Establish the 4:2:4 breath cycle as described on page 16. Use the Middle Pillar Exercise (see page 49) to build up colors, starting with Kether and proceeding down to Malkuth. Intone the Divine name as you build each sephira. This helps to establish it through the vibrating power of sound. Image the beam of white light connecting each of the spheres in turn: Kether to Da'ath, to Tiphareth, to Yesod, and finally to Malkuth. When the Middle Pillar is established, return your attention to Kether.

1. With an exhalation of breath, visualize a stream of brilliant white light passing down the left side of your body and aura into Malkuth, to a mental count of four.

2. Remain focused at Malkuth for a mental count of 2.

3. While inhaling to the count of four, image the stream of brilliant white light passing up the right side of your body and aura into Kether, which crowns your head.

4. Remain focused in Kether for a count of two.

5. Repeat: outgoing breath (4), Kether to Malkuth down the left side; hold in Malkuth (2); incoming breath (4), Malkuth to Kether up the right side; hold in Kether (2).

6. Repeat the cycle six times in all. It is important that you hold on to the idea that the stream of white light is passing through your body as well as your aura. This will ensure that the incoming cosmic energy circulates through all of your bodies (subtle and physical), enhancing them all.

Taking one sephira for a three-day period of meditation, build a short fantasy in which a positive aspect of that sephira is enacted. For example, in Geburah, visualize a group of people who are listless and apathetic. Introduce the energizing influence of Geburah to vitalize and invigorate them in a positive way. Or build a scenario consisting of a neglected orchard in which the fruit trees had been left for years, overcome with ivy and parasites, weeds rampant throughout the field. Bring in positive Geburic influence: The weeds are cut back, the trees pruned, decisions made regarding which trees can be saved and which are to be felled, the appropriate use of sharp tools and instruments to restore the orchard to productivity, the burning of dead wood, and the alchemical process of making compost from the pruned cuttings to recycle the released energy for nurturing future harvests of fruit.

Begin with Kether, spending three days on it. Then proceed to Chokmah, and so on, through to Malkuth. Do not include Da'ath in this particular exercise. End with the Qabalistic Cross and write an entry in your journal.

Using fantasy in this way enables you to make deeper connections with the sephiroth, to vitalize your intellectual study of them with emotion. In this way, both Hod (intellect/study) and Netzach (emotion/fantasy) compliment each other, and their synthesis brings about the potential for real knowledge. By perceiving the influences of the sephiroth in the visible, you prepare yourself to *know* them in the unseen.

RULING THE INNER KINGDOM

Nothing escapes the Principle of Cause and Effect, but there are many
planes of Causation, and one may use the laws of the higher
to overcome the laws of the lower.

—THE KYBALION

It is wise to reflect upon what you have learned. Some Qabalists make an annual discipline of looking back upon the previous year's accomplishments, achievements, transgressions (literally "missing the mark"), and failures. This taking stock is usually undertaken from the Winter Solstice (December 21st) to Candlemas (February 2nd) and forms the basis of their meditations during this time. This is a review of the greater solar cycle of one year, just as your daily Evening Review encompasses the lesser solar cycle of each day. It is during this annual review that you come to see just how far-reaching and potent the Evening Review Exercise is, and what a powerful practice it is for minimizing the purgation process that occurs after physical death.

In a deeper sense, you are always subconsciously processing something from past experience, observing the repetition of patterns of behavior and response, and liberating energy trapped in past hurts that once conditioned, but no longer serve you well. This reflection is not an indulgence in self-pity, neither is it an apportioning of blame onto others. It is a critical assessment of your progress toward the goals you set for yourself.

- Have those goals been achieved?
- If not, what has prevented you from achieving them?
- Are they still valid goals, or has deeper reflection led you to re-evaluate them?
- If so, what goals do you set for yourself now?
- What skills do you need to cultivate if those goals are to be achieved?

Microcosmically, self-reflection mirrors the eleventh path on the Tree, the relationship between Kether and Chokmah. Kether establishes the second sephira, Chokmah, and Chokmah, the sphere of wisdom, mirrors back to Kether as perfect self-reflection. In Chokmah, the One Life knows itself utterly. And it is from this perfect knowledge of infinite potentiality that the will to create arises.

In the economy of Providence, even transgression—failing to hit the mark—has its uses. For example, consider how, although experiences derived from transgression do not automatically result in wisdom, they certainly result in knowledge (Da'ath). This experiential knowledge may then lead on to a deeper understanding (Binah), resulting in more skillful means, and so, in due course, ripen into wisdom (Chokmah).

Once you have taken stock of yourself and your situation, you are in a position to go forward. The great value of self-reflection is that it heals fragmentation and so precipitates synthesis and integration. In the symbolism of Egypt, this is called harvesting the golden wheat of wisdom. Those who would travel high must travel light. By the practice of self-reflection, you can process heavy psychological baggage and allow yourself to carry your past experiences lightly—while still remaining in touch with them. You become like the Fool in tarot Key 0, who jauntily carries his bag of experiences attached to a staff resting on his shoulder.

We have spoken of the Most Holy One, who wears the whole magnificence of existence like a garment to give appearance to unmanifest reality, just as our spirits wear subtle and physical garments. We each create our own world by our own thinking, shaping the universe by our own subjective perceptions. How the world is seen depends upon the inner world of the individual who sees it. The universe—life—holds up a mirror to our inner states and reflects back to us what we send out.

We are linked with the whole, and may consciously choose, through alignment with its center and source, to become open channels through which the life-power may pour. The ability to mediate consciously the influence of the upper worlds, bringing it to bear upon a situation, opens up the possibility of profound change for all involved. This is one implication of the teaching, from *The Kybalion*, quoted at the beginning of the chapter. Because we are conscious, study, contemplation, and imagination help us to begin to understand the One's consciousness. This is not easy and happens, at first, only in splendid moments of illumination that increase as our capacity to understand deepens, until finally it becomes a permanent state of at-one-ment. When we become capable of taking part in the Eternal's consciousness—in its will, imagination, and bliss—we are aware of all the implications and subtleties of the whole. Then we play our part in the great cycle of being and nonbeing that turns forever.

There are men and women who have already achieved various degrees of the great unfoldment. They constitute what is often called in Qabalah, the Spiritual Israel. This vanguard of human evolution is also called the College of the Holy Spirit, the Communion of Saints, and the Great White Lodge. Some of its Asian titles are the *Vajra-Sangha* and the *Mahatmas*.

Sowing Seeds

Seed sentences are short phrases that are used to promote response from the deeper knowing of your spirit, your higher self, as when a piece of grit is introduced into an oyster in the hope that a pearl will develop. A seed sentence is meditated upon at odd moments—not in formal meditation sessions, but more as a gentle mulling-over in the mind. You turn it over until your subconscious accepts it, and begins to work upon it with associative ideas. Sometimes years pass before the meaning of a particular seed sentence becomes clear. Many of the advanced teachings are expressed as seed sentences. We have already received some in this book. The titles of most of the chapters are, in fact, seed sentences or phrases. Other examples are: All gods are One God; Fantasy is the ass that carries the Ark; As Above so Below, but after another manner; The Kingdom of Heaven is within you.

Catch Exercises

The following exercises are designed to facilitate shifts in consciousness to another of the many levels of awareness of which you are capable. They are called "catch exercises," since they lift you into an inner perception, yet do not sever you from physical reality. They "catch" moments of great awareness while you are immersed in the humdrum of everyday routine. It is through the regular practice of catch exercises that you acquire the skills to make these shifts in consciousness smoothly. As with all acquired skills, frequent practice will sow the seed into the fertile soil of your subconscious. When your subconscious has accepted the seed and worked upon it, results will begin to appear. In time, you are enabled to change your levels of perception, even in a crowded or distracting situation. When this skill is acquired, you can be used by Above as a lens through which the Inner Light may be brought to bear. This is one aspect of extending the Light.

The Noonday Salutation

The Noonday Salutation is one such catch exercise. It makes you aware of the Sun at its zenith and uses this imagery to open you to the forces of light that are being outpoured. Having realized this, you then use the altered state of consciousness to invoke the Divine blessing of peace upon the Earth.

You can incorporate the Noonday Salutation into your own daily disciplines. Its purpose is to expand awareness into a deeper perception of the present moment of time—the eternal Now. Its practice sows the seed of freeing you from your habitual perception of where and who you are, and places you within the context of the grand design. It also encourages your mind to extend its field of awareness, to see things from a greater perspective.

THE NOONDAY SALUTATION

Having prepared yourself for meditation using the opening Qabalistic Cross (see page 17), the relaxation exercise (see page 15), and the 4:2:4 breathing cycle (see page 16), perform the following visualization.

Become aware of where you are standing, where you are upon the planet's surface; in which building, in which city/town/countryside; on which island or land mass; on which continent; in which hemisphere of the planet called Earth. Extend your awareness to embrace the planet Earth in its relationship to the Sun, about which it orbits; in relationship to the other planets, moons, and satellites, all engaged in the circling dance of the solar system. Expand your awareness of the daystar orbiting—through stupendous distances and over huge measurements of time—the galactic center. Become aware of these magnificent and interdependent cycles . . . and of yourself, in existence at this very moment. Become aware of that which encompasses all, from the vast to the minute, upholding the totality in its all-embracing consciousness . . . Now!

Ablution

All meditations and rituals should be preceded by an ablution. This is a symbolic rite of purification. It has nothing whatsoever to do with physical hygiene. You make the act of ablution with the intention to purify yourself for the work ahead. It focuses, and so protects, you. Advanced and intensive ritual workings are preceded by total immersion.

ABLUTION EXERCISE

1. Turn on a water tap and pass each hand in turn under the running water.

2. Cup your hands together so they fill with water and bathe your face.

3. Speak the words from Psalm 121 with intention and the awareness of what you are doing, and why: "Thou shalt sprinkle me with hyssop, Oh Lord, and I shall be clean. Thou shalt wash me, and I will be whiter than snow."

4. While performing the physical actions, hold in your mind the idea of purification, of realignment with your Divine center.

The Rose upon the Cross

In the Latin form of the symbol of the cross, the bottom arm is longer than the other three, forming the six faces of an unfolded cube. The number six relates to the sixth sephira, Tiphareth, as does the golden color of the cross. Tiphareth is the "heart" of the Tree. Notice, as well, that the diagram of the Tree itself is an irregular hexagon, a six-sided figure. The spiritual experience of Tiphareth is a vision of the harmony of things.

The rose is sacred to Venus, the Roman form of the goddess of desire, and so to the sephira Netzach. The symbol of the rose, as used in the Mysteries, is depicted in a stylized manner—what is termed in heraldry a Tudor rose. The color and number of its petals vary according to the nature of the work. Here, we will use a five-petaled ruby-red rose.

And so, our glyph combines two symbols: one for the spirit or the higher self in Tiphareth, the other for the desire-nature of personality, attributed to Netzach. The joining of these two symbols forms the Rose-Cross, which symbolizes the conscious uniting of your desire-nature with your higher self. It is therefore a symbol of redemption—the raising of the personal to the transpersonal level of spirit. Also, because Tiphareth is Kether upon a lower arc, the Rose-Cross further signifies an unfolded personality, cocentered within the unconditional love of the higher self and receptive to the Divine.

This profound symbol is visualized as a square-ended Latin cross, golden like the sunlight reflecting off the gold metal. The five petals of the rose are vivid crimson, like a ruby. Upon the golden heart of the rose-flower, there delicately rests a single drop of dew, signifying *mezla*, grace, the dew of heaven. This dewdrop reflects *and refracts* the white brilliance.

Essentially, the Rose-Cross represents a sacred human—any person who consciously mediates Above to Below, one though whom the dark lead of physicality is irradiated by the golden light of the indwelling spirit. This is further amplified by the Divine name that is used in conjunction with this symbol in ritual: *Yeheshua*. This Divine name is formed of the letters of the Tetragrammaton—Yod, Heh, Vau, Heh—with the holy letter, Shin (representing the human spirit), centered within it. The symbol and the name together—through visual and auditory vibrations—open us to the reality they represent.

The Ritual of the Rose-Cross is a rite of power and protection. The power it channels is that of Tiphareth, the sacred heart of the universe. The protection it extends is that of the Holy Guardian Angel, the higher self who is at one with the universe.

This ritual is used to create a powerful yet harmonious sphere of energy. Some think that harmony is a weak, almost passive, quality. However, when you think of it as balance in this context, you gain insight into the skill, precision, and strength required to balance opposing forces and qualities and hold them in perfect integrated harmony. This ritual technique is wisely used for creating the ideal conditions for meditation and for healing. It can also be used to balance out atmospheres when strong, negative emotions have been discharged or when conflicts or arguments have occurred. Where debilitating illness has been present, the healing and redemptive influence of Tiphareth may be invoked through working the Ritual of the Rose-Cross. You may also utilize this ritual formula subjectively, to center yourself and regain harmony and inner poise.

In this respect, the Ritual of the Rose-Cross is more useful and constructive than the more widely known Banishing Pentagram Ritual. New practitioners of occultism fall too easily into the trap of banishing everything in sight. It feeds their inherent power complexes. Being skillful, being adept, means knowing which tool will perform each task most effectively. The Banishing Pentagram Ritual has all the grace of steel wool; it literally scours an atmosphere clean. The result is a pure, sterile inner space. It removes all impressions from the place where it is performed, leaving it like a blank, colorless canvas. It is for this very reason that the Banishing Pentagram is worked before consecrations, because it does remove *everything*—good, bad, and indifferent. However, sterile atmospheres are not conducive to soul growth. They are necessary for certain magical operations, but are quite unproductive for inner nourishment.

Consider a home in which an argument has occurred. Do you banish everything, including the trace of every thought and act of love, of nurture, and of refuge. Or do you invoke the redemptive harmony of the sphere of Tiphareth, the Sun, and thereby transmute the shadows and reinforce all the positive qualities? Consider a hospital room or ward. Do you banish everything, including the traces of the selfless work of the healthcare staff, the councilors and spiritual ministers, the ennobling examples of human courage in the face of adversity, let alone the ongoing work of the angels of healing? Or do you invoke the influence of Tiphareth to enfold the area, augmenting the healing that takes place within its confines and uniting your own efforts with the other healers, both human and angelic?

You can perform the Ritual of the Rose-Cross before your meditation session and then meditate within its sphere, or perform it at some other

81

time in the day. It is best, at first, to do the ritual physically in your meditation space, thus impregnating that space with the influence of Tiphareth and of your real self. For the purposes of meditation and ritual, we have assumed that your altar faces east. This may be arbitrary, but if you so intend and so act, it *will* face east in your inner space.

THE RITUAL OF THE ROSE-CROSS

Having performed the Ablution Exercise (see page 78), light the lamp on your altar, mentally acknowledging that it represents the Divine presence within you.

1. Stand in the center of your sacred space, facing east (your altar).

2. Perform the opening Qabalistic Cross (see page 17).

3. Go to the southeast corner of your space and trace a large Calvary Cross, vertical line first, then the horizontal line.

4. Trace a clockwise circle upon the center of the cross. Do this quite rapidly, as if setting a top spinning, forming thereby a vortex of force oriented by the cross.

5. Point to the center of the circle (and cross) and intone or chant the Divine name: *Yeheshua.* As you do so, visualize the entire symbol taking on the full form as described above: gold cross, ruby rose, and sparkling dewdrop.

6. With your arm outstretched before you, go to the southwest and repeat the tracing, intoning, and visualization.

7. With your arm outstretched before you, go to the northwest and repeat the tracing, intoning, and visualization.

8. With your arm outstretched arm before you, go to the north-east and repeat the tracing, intoning, and visualization.

9. Complete the circumambulation by returning to the southeast, making the circle complete by pointing to the center of the original Rose-Cross.

10. Return to the center and face east.

11. Raise your arm and build a Rose-Cross above you in the same manner as before.

12. With your arm outstretched above you, go to the northwest and bring your hand down to point to the center of the symbol. There is no need to retrace it or recall the name.

13. Turn your right shoulder so you are facing southeast. With your arm outstretched below you, retrace your steps to the center of the space and formulate the symbol under your feet in the center, tracing, intoning, and visualizing.

13. Complete the vertical circle by returning to the southeast, with your arm stretched down. Bring your arm up to point to the center of the Rose-Cross already established there.

14. Raising your arm again, return to the center and focus on the Rose-Cross above your head.

15. Vibrate the name to commence the third circle. There is no need to retrace the symbol.

16. Trace a circle down to the northeast.

17. Trace under the floor to link up with the Rose-Cross beneath your feet in the center.

18. Trace the circle up to southwest Rose-Cross.

19. Complete the sphere by returning to the center, linking up to the Rose-Cross above you.

20. Make yourself the Rose-Cross by performing the closing Qabalistic Cross. Dwell on the idea that your personality is the flower grown and cultivated by the golden higher self to catch the dew of heaven. Strongly visualize yourself surrounded by the network of six Rose-Crosses—around, above, and beneath you—all connected by the three unbroken rings of golden light.

21. Meditate upon the significance of the ritual.

BUILDING THE TREE OF LIFE EXERCISE

This exercise will help to prepare you for the following Interwoven Light Exercises. Perform the Ritual of the Rose-Cross (see page 82) once a day for six days. Before you begin this exercise, perform the opening Qabalistic Cross (see page 17), then the relaxation exercise on page 15. Establish the 4:2:4 breath cycle, repeating it at least ten times.

1. Build up the Middle Pillar in the colors of the Queen scale, intoning the Divine names of the sephiroth.

2. Once this is established, start building the sephiroth of the side pillars. This may be done in easy stages—Kether on the first day, Chokmah on the second, and so on. You may find it a useful aid for memory to build Kether on the first day, Kether and Chokmah on the next, Kether, Chokmah, and Binah on the next, and so on. Do not add another sephira until the previous

84

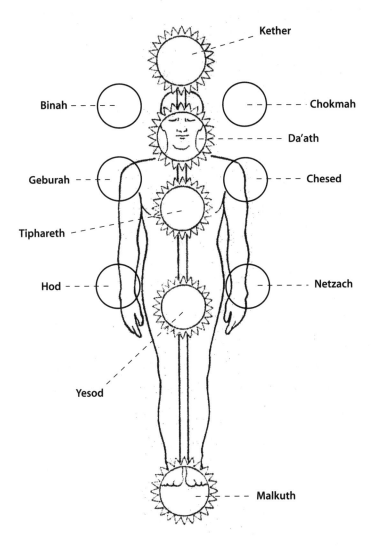

Figure 6. Building the Tree of Life.

ones can be formulated with ease. Use figure 6 (page 85) to determine their positions in relation to your physical body.

3. Visualize Kether as a sphere of white incandescence (like burning magnesium) upon your head and slightly interpenetrating the crown of your skull.

4. Visualize Chokmah in pale gray on the left side of your head.

5. See Binah in deepest indigo (or black) upon the right.

6. Visualize Da'ath as lavender, encompassing your throat and face.

7. Chesed should appear at your left shoulder and upper arm, in royal blue.

8. Geburah will correspond to the same position on your right, in scarlet.

9. See Tiphareth encompassing your heart and solar plexus, and as golden yellow in color.

10. Netzach should appear in emerald green at your left hip.

11. Make Hod bright orange, on your right hip.

12. Place Yesod, in violet, at your genitals.

13. Malkuth should encompass your ankles and feet with its fourfold coloration of citrine, olive, russet, and dark indigo.

When the sephiroth are established and called to mind with ease, image the twenty-two paths that unite them in white light. Visualizing the sephiroth and paths of the Tree of Life may be used at odd moments during the day as a catch exercise.

INTERWOVEN LIGHT EXERCISES

Once you have gained some proficiency in establishing the Tree within your aura, continue with the series of exercises known collectively as the Interwoven Light Exercises. These are graduated exercises designed to set up certain currents of energy in the sphere of sensation (the bodies, physical and subtle, and the various levels of the aura) and to bring these forces through into the physical levels. You began the first stage of the Interwoven Light Exercises in chapter 3 with the Middle Pillar Visualization (see page 47), drawing energy from Kether, down the left-hand side of your body and aura into Malkuth on an exhaled breath to the count of four. Then, on the inhaled breath, you drew the energy up from Malkuth, through the right-hand side of your body and aura, and into Kether. The next two stages of the Interwoven Light Exercises are as follows:

1. Establish rhythmic breathing (see page 16), and perform the Middle Pillar Exercise (see page 49)

2. Focus upon the crown center of Kether. Image it as revolving rapidly, a whirling sphere of white brilliance, drawing into itself energy from the universe and making it available for immediate human use.

3. With an exhalation, direct the white energy to Malkuth, down the front of your body and aura. Remain focused in Malkuth for a count of two.

4. With inhaled breath, let the light ascend through the back of your body and aura, returning into the crown.

5. Focus in Kether for a count of two, then recommence the cycle.

This exercise should be performed for at least six full cycles. Do not be alarmed when you begin to feel physical sensations like goose bumps or tingling. This is just your physical body responding to the inflow of energy. You will find that this exercise has the effect of invigorating you with the vital current of life.

After completing this exercise, rest in the resultant sense of calmness, vitality, and well-being. Allow the life-force to nourish you on all levels. Then close with the Qabalistic Cross and write up your notes.

Continue this exercise for two weeks, then move on to the next phase of Interwoven Light exercises.

1. Perform the opening Qabalistic Cross (see page 17) and establish rhythmic breathing and the Middle Pillar as before.

2. Circulate the light from Kether to Malkuth, down and up the sides of your sphere of sensation, for at least six full cycles.

3. Circulate the energy from Kether to Malkuth, down the front and up the back of your sphere of sensation, for at least six full cycles.

4. Focus on Malkuth and visualize white light, in a broad band, ascending as a spiral. Image the spiral arising from beneath your right foot, passing behind your left calf, around across your right thigh, and so on. This results in a spiral of white light arising in a clockwise direction from Malkuth to Kether. The spiral should enfold your entire sphere of sensation (aura and body) within its white brilliance.

5. Use the lines of descent and ascent from the first two stages of the Interwoven Light exercise to give you a sense of the ovoid

of the aura, about which the rising spiral coils. Let the spiral arise on an inhalation to a count of four.

6. Focus in Kether for a count of two, then image energy streaming from Kether directly to Malkuth for an exhaled count of four.

7. Focus on Malkuth for a count of two, then cause the spiral to ascend to Kether on a count of four.

Perform this exercise for at least six full cycles. When finished, gently dwell in the ovoid of white light. Close with the Qabalistic Cross and write up your notes.

6

A PILLAR OF GLORY

Malkuth causes an Influence to flow from the Prince of the Countenances

—SEPHER YETZIRAH

A lbert Pike, an authority on Freemasonry, wrote, in his book *Morals and Dogma of the Ancient and Accepted Scottish Rite:*

> One is filled with admiration, on penetrating into the Sanctuary of the Qabalah, at seeing a doctrine so logical, so simple, and at the same time so absolute. The necessary union of ideas and signs, the consecration of the most fundamental realities by the primitive characters; the Trinity of Words, Letters and Numbers; a philosophy simple as the alphabet, profound and infinite as the Word; theorems more complete and luminous than those of Pythagoras; a theology summed up by the counting of one's fingers; an Infinite which can be held in the hollow of an infant's hand; ten cyphers and twenty-two letters, a triangle, a square and a circle,—these are all the elements of the Qabalah. These are the elementary principles of the written word, reflection of that spoken Word that created the world![7]

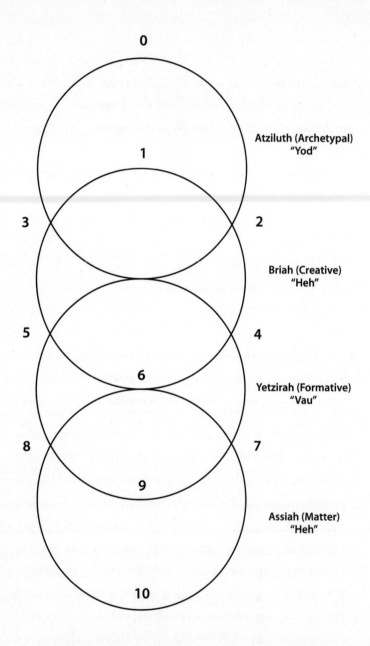

Figure 7. The Four Worlds and Their Correspondences.

The Qabalah teaches that existence is comprised of four worlds. Here, the word "world" bears its traditional meaning and does not refer to a planet located somewhere in space. It refers, rather, to a realm of a particular mode of Divine activity. Each world emanates, or proceeds, from the one before it, and gives rise to the one following it (see figure 7, page 92).

In each world, the Divine engages in more and more complex relationships, and yet remains indivisibly One.

The scheme of the Four Worlds helps you to grasp how the One Thing immerses itself in multiplicity—how one substance, pure mental energy, becomes a multitude of galaxies, stars, planets, and beings both physical and nonphysical. Each world represents a slowing down of the vibratory frequency of the Divine radiance, until it solidifies as physical forms. The Four Worlds are realms of the Divine, spiritual (mental), astral (psychological), and physical. We can use a model of light, color, sound, and substance. Each human being contains within his or her totality a vehicle corresponding to, and functioning in, each of the Four Worlds. This is our heritage as expressions for God within existence.

Atziluth

The first world is named Atziluth, the Hebrew word for emanation. Its root also means "to stand near." This is the world of archetypes, where all that is willed to come into subsequent existence is held in potential. Atziluth corresponds to the letter Yod of the Tetragrammaton, *Yod-Heh-Vau-Heh*, and the element of fire. In tarot, it is symbolized by the kings of the four suits of the Minor Arcana. In ceremonial workings, the Atzilutic world is invoked by the names of God, in which the Divine attributes are embodied.

Atziluth is the perfect, unchanging world. It is what is meant by the term "world without end," used at the end of many invocations and prayers—indeed, used in the Qabalistic Cross. Atziluth is the world of divinity, also called in tradition the world of Divine lights and the glory of God, for it permeates the lower worlds as an unseen radiance. Within Atziluth, the Tree of Life is the unchanging model of perfection. Here, the sephiroth are the ten aspects of reality, forming the mirror of God. The Tree in Atziluth is sometimes called the Tree of Holy Apples. It is from the world of Atziluth that the Divine spark—the real self—of every man and woman comes, and to which all shall return.

Briah

From the Heart of all Brightness, the Tiphareth of Atziluth, emerges the second realm, Briah, the world of creation. Here, one step removed from the Divine unity, time is called forth out of eternity. The great universal impulses of expansion, contraction, and balance come into being. The great cycles that will affect all subsequent existence have their basis in Briah. In Briah, the Divine archetypes of Atziluth are translated into spiritual ideals. This is the world of pure spirits, the great archangels who are the Princes of Heaven and who oversee the millions of cosmic processes. This world is also the natural realm of the higher self, the abode of your immortal spirit, which acts as a vessel for the Divine spark in the cosmic dimension of heaven. Some metaphysical traditions refer to this world as the mental level. In Briah are the halls of heaven, spiritual states of ascending refinement, entered by those who seek to serve God. Here also, are the deep inner-plane temples, orders, and schools, gathered about those members of the Great Council—the College of the Holy Spirit— who teach evolving humanity. Presiding over all is Metatron, the first self-realized and perfected human, who is chief of the archangels, at the Kether of Briah, which is simultaneously the Tiphareth of Atziluth.

Briah corresponds to the first Heh of the Tetragrammaton, to the element of air, and is represented by the four queen cards of tarot.

Yetzirah

The third realm, *Olham ha Yetzirah,* the world of Yetzirah, emanates from the Tiphareth of Briah. Yetzirah means "formation." Macrocosmically, this is the astral world; microcosmically, it is the psychological world. In Yetzirah are all the astral matrices that are the templates of physical form.

A physical body is in a continuous state of flux, since it is composed of cells that are constantly passing through their cycle of birth, generation, decay, and death. Absorption and elimination are continuous. It is the astral image of the body that defines and maintains the shape and cohesiveness of physical matter. Everything that appears physically, first manifests in Yetzirah as an astral form; one of the titles of this realm is the Treasure House of Images.

All forms, no matter how spiritual in appearance, are of the world of Yetzirah. Any perception, received in vision or dream, of Briah or even Atziluth is clothed in the forms of Yetzirah. It is one thing to perceive an astral form, but quite another thing to *know* the spiritual reality that the form represents.

The world of Yetzirah is the realm of the angels, those ministering spirits who keep the universe ticking over, who are ceaselessly engaged in the incalculable number of functions that existence needs to continue—natural rhythms, planetary cycles, changing climates, all the complexities of the interweaving dance ranging from the star to the atom.

Yetzirah is, for humanity, the emotional and psychological dimension, the place of the psyche, or incarnate soul, and the astral vehicle. And it is the world of the various abodes where discarnate humans dwell—the varying degrees of paradise and hell that mirror a person's interior state.

The letter Vau of the Tetragrammaton corresponds to Yetzirah, the element of water, and the minor tarot cards of the knights of the four suits.

Assiah

The fourth realm is *Assiah*, the world of action, the natural world. Macrocosmically, the entire physical universe and all incarnate existence composes Assiah. Microcosmically, it is the physical body. Assiah is the densest of the Four Worlds, the most limited and complex, subjected to the greatest number of laws; yet it is the willed result of all that has gone before. It is destined to manifest the Divine glory within time and space. It is said: "The earth shall be full of the glory of God as the waters cover the sea"; and "In my flesh shall I see God."

The final Heh of the Tetragrammaton represents Assiah and the element of earth. In tarot, it is signified by the Pages of Wands, Swords, Cups, and Pentacles.

Unity

The Four Worlds interpenetrate the whole of existence. Although we have briefly looked at them separately, they are in fact fully present, since they are four modes of the activity of the One Reality. They are *not* four separate realities.

To give an analogy, let us take water. Below the freezing point, water becomes a solid substance, ice. Between the freezing and boiling points, water is a fluid. Above the boiling point, water becomes gaseous as steam. Yet, in each of these three stages, water remains composed of atoms of hydrogen and oxygen. Atoms are particles of energy orbiting a nucleus of radiant light. Ice corresponds to Assiah, fluid to Yetzirah, steam to Briah, and the essential energy to Atziluth.

Let us take the sephira of Kether, in its aspects through the Four Worlds. In Atziluth, Kether may be thought of as the idea of Limitless Light in whirling motion at a central point. In Briah, this gives rise to the ideal of all beings crowned with light. In Yetzirah, Kether is an actual center of vortical motion in the etheric level. This formulates as the crown chakra in the subtle bodies. In Assiah, Kether is a condensation of physical, radiant energy at a point, whether it be the nucleus of an atom or the star of a planetary system. For us on Earth, our Sun is the Kether of this world system. In the human physical body, Kether is the pineal gland.

An incarnate human being exists in all four worlds. In Isaiah we read: "I called him (Atziluth), I created him (Briah), I formed him (Yetzirah), I made him (Assiah)." The Middle Pillar may be used as a preliminary tool for contemplating the Four Worlds: Kether corresponding to Atziluth, Tiphareth to Briah, Yetzirah to Yesod, and Assiah to Malkuth.

Everything that is comes from Above. Take a chair as an illustration. In the world of Atziluth comes forth the archetype of a seated human being. This archetype resonates in Briah, where the received Divine idea is expressed by the spiritual ideal of "chair"—the prototype of all chairs that will ever be, from thrones to milking stools. The impulse of the Briatic proto-chair reverberates into Yetzirah, where it is multiplied and diversified into the designs and forms of many chairs. Human craftsmen, who by their training are keyed into the concept of furniture, receive the astral impressions from Yetzirah and, by their skill, fashion physical chairs in Assiah.

Of course it is not quite as simple as that; a master craftsman does in fact make alterations to design in the Yetziratic world. Human consciousness can and does cause change and adjustment in the upper worlds. For humans have the potential to focus and function in all the worlds.

This introduction to the Qabalistic teaching on the Four Worlds prepares you for the final stage of the Interwoven Light Exercises. Many advanced students fail to comprehend the essentials of this technique and, as a consequence, often, many years later, have to return to this foundation stage and relearn and reapply it.

Like all the preceding stages of the Interwoven Light Exercises, the Fountain Breath Exercise links the movement of radiant energy with that of breath, until they become a conditioned reflex. By practicing it with intention, your subconscious accepts the linkage and the energy-breath pattern becomes automatic. The pitfall for many practitioners is the belief (and therefore the willed intention) that the white brilliance circulated in the exercise is only etheric or astral energy. What we have tried to transmit, by teaching at this stage the preliminaries of the Four Worlds, is that, just as the worlds interpenetrate one another, *so too do our inner vehicles.* Just as One Force flows through all the worlds, so too one synthesizing power can flow throughout your entire being.

Although, diagrammatically, the Four Worlds are often portrayed as descending or ascending one from another, in fact they are within each other, rather like the Russian matrushka doll we mentioned before. The etheric, astral, mental, and spiritual bodies occupy the same space as the physical body. In every place, the Four Worlds are present. This is as true of the Microcosm as it is of the Macrocosm. This needs to be fully grasped so that, when you perform the Interwoven Light Exercises, you know and make the intention that the white brilliance will irradiate you on *all* levels.

And what is the white brilliance brought into your sphere of sensation and moved in accordance with breath? It is the dew of heaven, *mezla*, the Limitless Light itself. And how are you enabled to draw down heaven's dew? Because, as the seed-sentence at the beginning of this chapters says: (We) Malkuth (may) cause an influence to flow from the Prince of the Countenances (Kether).

Before describing the Fountain Breath Exercise itself, I offer the following alchemical extract by Artephius for meditation. Note here that the author veils the Limitless Light under the name "water of life":

> This *aqua vitae*, or water of life being rightly ordered . . . It is the royal fountain in which the King (Sol) and Queen (Luna) bathe themselves . . . and the Spirit is incorporated with the Body, and made one with it.[8]

THE FOUNTAIN BREATH EXERCISE

To perform the Fountain Breath Exercise, first complete the preceding stages of the Interwoven Light Exercises given on pages 87–89. Then focus your consciousness upon the crown center of Kether.

1. With the exhaled breath, to a count of 4, image Kether as a fountain of pure white brilliance that outpours an incandescent torrent down through your entire body and aura, that pools in the Malkuth center at your feet.

2. Focus your attention on Malkuth for a count of 2.

3. With the inhaled breath, on a count of 4, see a column of white light tinged with rainbow colors ascend from Malkuth, through Yesod, Tiphareth, and Da'ath, and into the white sphere of Kether.

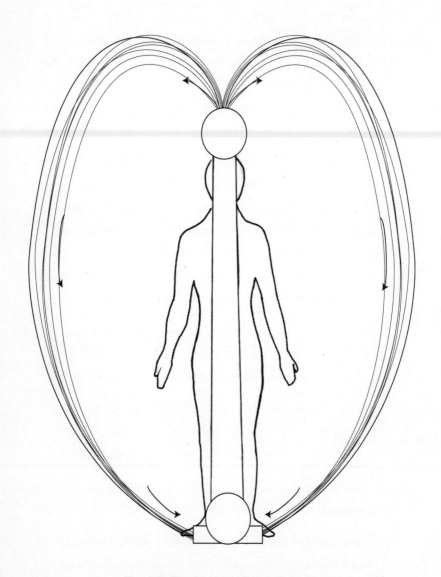

Figure 8. The Fountain Breath Exercise.

4. Hold your focus on Kether for a further count of 2.

5. With the next exhalation, Kether fountains the white brilliance again, down into Malkuth.

6. Pause and, with the inhalation, see the white column ascend through the Middle Pillar back to the crown.

Continue this for approximately ten times (see figure 8, page 100).

Divine grace flows through all four worlds. It is the animating force of everything, and the root substance of all form. Sometimes, it is imaged as fiery sweat (the "water that burns"), sometimes as oil, sometimes as manna, the bread that sustains us while in exile. This is why food plays an important part in the rituals of many religions; spirit nourishes and sustains existence. This is what Jesus meant when he taught people to pray, saying: "give us this day our daily bread." Beyond existence—beyond Kether—this One Power is termed the Limitless Light; within existence, it is named *chaiah*, the life force. Israel Regardie wrote of it:

> The force of life is infinite; we are saturated, permeated through and through with this spiritual force, this energy. It constitutes our higher self, it is our link with Godhead, it is God within us. Every molecule of our physical system is soaked with the dynamic energy of this force; each cell in our body contains it in abundance.[9]

It is this One Force that you consciously access in the Interwoven Light Exercises. You are working for an increase of grace, to bring forth the fruits of the spirit. And you open yourself to it on all levels: spiritual, mental, emotional, and physical. Apart from the great benefit this exercise has in helping you to center down for meditation, it is also of tremendous help in your work of regeneration, in healing psychological and physical disease. I recommend Israel Regardie's book *The Art of True Healing* for those who wish to read further.

Although there are other refinements of these exercises used in specialized areas of work, what has been given contains the foundation for the work of regeneration.

Concerning Adam Qadmon

The Tree in Atziluth, the image of the Divine, is called Adam Qadmon. It is a poetic image of the primordial human surrounded by fiery brightness that the prophet Ezekial saw upon the throne of heaven, riding the chariot drawn by the four holy creatures. The sephiroth are the various parts of the body of Adam Qadmon; their arrangement is the same as in figure 6 (see page 85) and as that used for the Interwoven Light Exercises. Adam Qadmon is androgynous, the perfect amalgam of female and male. "Adam" is a technical Mystery term used as a generic noun for all humanity. So Adam Qadmon is the supernal image in the mind of the Absolute of the total human life-wave, whose purpose is to reflect the Divine back to itself so that God may behold God. Adam Qadmon is the *Logos* or "Word" of Hellenistic philosophy, the Cosmic Christ of esoteric Christianity, "the express image of the brightness of the Father's Glory."

The self of the self—*Yechidah*, the Divine spark of every single man and woman, incarnate or discarnate—is a cell of the body of Adam Qadmon. In a real sense, the potential of humanity was collectively involved in the creation and formation of the lower worlds. Everything that has come into being upon this planet and elsewhere in the universe came through the mediation of Divine humanity, of Adam Qadmon. Before time began, humanity, as a homogeneous whole, was involved in the work of cocreation. Later, when the physical universe was manifest, we were given the opportunity to continue as cocreators with the Eternal, but now as self-conscious units, as individuals. So it is said in the Mysteries: "By Man will the Great Work be completed."

In Hindu cosmology, there is the teaching of the Days and Nights of Brahma—a concept of vast aeons of time wherein universes are created and sustained, followed by a corresponding period when all returns to the Divine source. Qabalah holds the same teaching, known as a *shemittah,* or great cosmic cycle. In each day of Brahma, new factors are willed into being by the Eternal One, to be worked out in the worlds and their creatures. Thus the days are not a mere repetition of each other, but each day is a new adventure of the spirit in which original, and hitherto unknown, aspects of the infinite One come into manifestation.

This is shown in tarot by Key 0, the Fool, a pictorial image of Adam Qadmon. The peaks of the mountain range in the background of this card represent previous days of Brahma. The androgynous Fool carries a staff from which hangs a red wallet. The wallet's flap bears the symbol of the all-seeing eye, has ten stitches for the sephiroth, and is adorned with the image of an eagle. The eagle is the bird of Jupiter, corresponding to Chesed, and signifies wealth. What is portrayed here is the Fool going forth once more in the dawn of a new day, carrying with him all the experiences gleaned by the One Life-Power in its previous days of manifestation. Nothing is ever lost; anything that reflects the good, the beautiful, and the true—however humbly—is held forever in the mind of God.

At the end of a day of Brahma, when the shemittah is completed, the worlds of Assiah, Yetzirah, and Briah are withdrawn back into the radiance of Atziluth that gave them birth. This is the Great Jubilee, when all "enter upon the joy of their Lord." After a subsequent night of Brahma, the creative *fiat* will sound once again and a new day will dawn, when once again the morning stars will sing together and all the sons of God will shout for joy. And once more, we will go forth forming worlds anew, building the new wonders shown on the trestle board of the Grand Architect of the Universe.

This extract may help you to contemplate Adam Qadmon:

[The seer] finds himself amid a company of innumerable beings, manifestly Divine; for they are the Angels and Archangels, Principalities and Powers, and all the hierarchy of the Heavens. Pressing on, through these towards the center, he next finds himself in the presence of a light so intolerable in its lustre as wellnigh to beat him back from further quest.

Enshrined in this light is a Form radiant and glorious beyond all power of expression. For it is "made of the Substance of Light"; and the form is that of the "Only Begotten," the Logos, the Idea, the Manifestor of God . . . the Lord Adonai. From the right hand upraised in attitude indicative of will and command, proceeds, as a stream of living force, the Holy Life and Substance whereby and whereof Creation consists. With the left hand, depressed and open as in an attitude of recall, the stream is indrawn, and Creation is sustained and redeemed. Thus projecting and recalling, expanding and contracting, Adonai fulfils the functions expressed in the mystical formula *Solve et Coagula*. And as in this, so also in constitution and form, Adonai is dual, comprising the two modes of humanity, and appearing to the beholder alternately masculine and feminine according as the function exercised is of the man or of the woman, and is centrifugal or centripetal.[10]

Since each human is a cell in the body of Adam Qadmon, each acts, consciously or unconsciously, as eyes and ears for the Divine. Through humanity, the Most Holy One experiences creation in detail. It follows, then, that a human being may consciously choose to dedicate him- or herself to be an instrument for the Divine.

This being the case, consider the sephiroth of the Middle Pillar from the viewpoint of the Divine acting through the personal spheres of such a dedicated man or woman. Table 4 shows the words of power and dedication involved in this process.

Table 4. The Sephiroth of the Middle Pillar
Acting through Personal Dedication

SEPHIRA	DIVINE VIEWPOINT	PERSONAL DEDICATION
Kether	Eheieh	I am
Da'ath	Yahveh-Elohim	I speak
Tiphareth	Yahveh Eloah ve Da'ath	I love
Yesod	Shaddai El Chai	I create
Malkuth	Adonai h'Aretz	I bless

CHANTING THE TREE EXERCISE

Begin by performing the opening Qabalistic Cross (see page 17) and the relaxation exercise on page 15. Establish the 4:2:4 breathing cycle (see page 16). Build the Middle Pillar (see page 16), in the Queen color scale of Briah. Circulate the white brilliance through your body and aura, both sides, front and back, for at least six complete circuits. Then perform the Fountain Breath Exercise (see page 99) for approximately five minutes.

1. Visualize the sephiroth of the side pillars within your sphere of sensation. See them as being formed of brilliant white light. Use the image of the Lightning Flash (see pages 42–43) to help you establish the pillars, weaving them with the already established spheres of the Middle Pillar. Thus: Kether, Chokmah, Binah, Da'ath, Chesed, Geburah, Tiphareth, Netzach, Hod, Yesod, and Malkuth.

2. On each day, will one of the sephiroth to radiate in the color scale of Briah (the Queen scale), intoning the Divine name of the sephira to trigger this change of color. Chokmah, *Yah*; Binah, *Elohim*; Chesed, *El*; Geburah, *Elohim-Gibor*; Netzach, *Yahveh-Tzabaoth*; Hod, *Elohim-Tzabaoth*. Use the chart of the Tree above your altar to assist you.

3. Start with Kether. Then, for two days, work on Chokmah, then two days on Binah, and so on. As you descend the Tree, ensure that you maintain the visualization of the preceding sephiroth in color. Do not let them slip back into white, so that, by the time you reach Malkuth, you can hold the entire Tree in the Queen scale.

4. When you have accomplished this, use whatever days remain for the cycle (thirty days) to strengthen the image. Move your consciousness up and down the Lightning Flash until you become flexible. This is a good foundation exercise for mental agility.

5. Finish by visualizing, for a while, the entire Tree within your aura. Picture the sephiroth in the Queen scale, and the connecting paths in white light. This serves as a powerful image of integrated relationship upon all levels of being.

Close the session with the closing Qabalistic Cross and write up your notes in your journal.

THE GREAT WORK

God is your mirror in which you contemplate yourself and you are His
mirror in which He contemplates His Divine attributes.

—IBN ARABI

It may seem strange to some people when I say that spiritual and magical formulae can have adverse side effects. All forces, although Divine in origin and essential nature, are capable of being misused by humankind. Any formula is a double-edged sword that can wound the very person who seeks to wield it. On the blade of a sword in Arthurian legend, it is written: "He who draws me from the Stone must master me or I will master him."

The Fountain Breath Exercise (see page 99) is just such a formula. The white brilliance drawn down through the Kether center in this exercise partakes of the nature of Kether. This influence, like Kether, is the primal unity. So the white brilliance is integrating in nature; it brings all the other sephiroth in your subjective Tree into harmonious alignment with it. Anything that obstructs this unifying and life-enhancing influence is dissolved, transformed, or rejected. Whether the obstructions are psychological (fears or complexes) or whether they are physical defects at the cellular level, these obstacles will be dissolved and transmuted.

In the case of obstructions in the psyche, as they become the focus for the descending influence from the superconscious level, they are "lit up" and brought to the surface of consciousness. Once upon the screen of self-consciousness, they are dissolved by attention, and the emotional/psychic energy that was trapped in them (sometimes for many years) is liberated. The released energy is then able to flow in a balanced way along the channels of psychological association with the sephiroth that have been built by your meditations.

Physical obstructions to the descending light are either dissolved or ejected, and finer matter replaced in the physical organism, enabling the physical body to resonate more closely to the influence's vibration. The body of an adept is not very different in outward appearance; the difference lies in the spectrum of forces to which it can resonate, and the unfoldment of organs that are dormant in most people. The greater the refinement of the vehicle, the more life-power it can transmit. The Great One who holds the mediating office for humankind in his or her time is sometimes referred to as the Lamp of the Shekinah, and also as the Anointed of the Light.

Possible Effects

The most common problem that exposes practitioners to risk is incompetence. You may try to use a technique for which you are unfit, or for which you lack the necessary development or training. Conversely, even if you are competent enough, you may use a formula lazily or arrogantly and consequently get burned. Still, burning your fingers does give you a healthy respect for the ways of power. An ounce of experience is worth a ton of theory.

There are three dangers you may risk when working the Fountain Breath Exercise. One is physical, one emotional (astral), and one mental (spiritual). The physical and emotional dangers are not too problematic once you understand their root cause; you must always remain alert, however, for the third, the mental.

Physical Effects

In some cases, the Fountain Breath Exercise provokes physical symptoms like minor aches and pains, skin rashes and spots, and occasional digestive disorders. Now this appears to be at variance with the health-enhancing claims I made for this technique. None of these symptoms last for very long, but if they do, you should consult a doctor. They are caused by the inflowing light prompting your physical body to expel toxins from your system, rather like clearing a blocked drainpipe. The life-power raises the vibratory rate of your inner vehicles and consequently brings about a refinement of the quality of matter that comprises your physical body. You may also find that, if you have refrained from meditating for a considerable period, this elimination process may recur (usually for a much shorter time) while you get back into your stride. The other aspect of this phenomenon is a rebellious lower self, which uses every trick it can to break the new habit of self-discipline. There is a phase in interior work where the lower self makes a bid for freedom. Generating emotional and/or physical irritations or fatigue are part of the personality's arsenal. But if you quietly and steadily persist, the symptoms will pass. Such are the dubious joys of embodiment.

Emotional Effects

The emotional problem you risk is called The Dark Night of the Soul.

This is well known to mystics and contemplatives. It is a feeling of utter failure, unworthiness, and an intense depression of spirits. It is caused, in part, by nervous overstrain, by carrying a higher voltage than you are used to. The remedy is to cut down for a while on the formative aspect of meditation (thought-form visualization) and to prolong the relaxation aspect; just build up the Tree of Life and bathe in the radiance flowing through Kether. The other cause of this depression is the inescapable contrast between the darkness of the material plane and the glories of the higher worlds. But you can put even this to good use. You see in the inner worlds the glories of existence; you encounter spirits of light, wisdom, and compassion, and see what humankind could be. You may even be graced with a glimpse of the Heart of all Brightness. Then, as you turn to the outer plane of physicality, you see the suffering, the cruelty, the ignorance that humankind inflicts upon itself and upon others. This contrast, as stark as the black and white squares of the temple's pavement, can only spur you to renew your efforts to serve the will of heaven and so to help transform the physical world of action and the elements (Assiah) into a paradise on Earth, in which the presence of the Eternal is known by every incarnate being.

Spiritual Effects

The spiritual risk is the greatest of all. I repeat myself deliberately when I say that you must always be on the lookout for this in the Work. It is the Luciferic vice of *hubris*, or spiritual pride, which is attributed, with good reason, to Tiphareth. As the white brilliance is drawn through the crown center and into your sphere of sensation, your personalities can easily become inflated. The white brilliance is the all-pervading life-force, and your contact with it, via the Fountain Breath Exercise, brings sensations of power and clarity of perception that tend to make you feel greater than you are. This can so easily lead to an attitude of self-importance or superiority. This problem is very common among people who attempt to work rituals without the prerequisite training. It arises because of the personality's tendency to regard anything coming into its orbit as its own personal possession. The cause of this is your identification with your false ego, your inaccurate belief that the personality is the true "I"— hence your need to align yourself consciously with the true "I am," the One Reality.

Why is the Fountain Breath Exercise able to stir up the physical, psychic, and spiritual levels? The answer to this lies in the Qabalistic teaching on the Four Worlds that we discussed in the previous chapter. When the Tree of Life is portrayed in each of the Four Worlds, each "World Tree" interfaces with the one above and the one below it. The greater countenance of Assiah (Kether, Chokmah, Binah, Da'ath, and Tiphareth) interfaces with the lesser countenance of Yetzirah (Tiphareth, Netzach, Hod, Yesod, and Malkuth). This continues throughout the extended Tree of Life—called Jacob's Ladder. So the greater-countenance sephiroth of a lower world is simultaneously the lesser countenance of the world above it: Assiah to Yetzirah; Yetzirah to Briah; and Briah to Atziluth.

Take the interface between the worlds of Assiah (physicality) and Yetzirah (astral/psychological) as an example. The Kether, Chokmah, Binah, Da'ath, and Tiphareth of Assiah are simultaneously the Tiphareth, Netzach, Hod, Yesod, and Malkuth of Yetzirah. This interface is observable. Emotions (Yetzirah) do generate physical sensation: goose bumps, tears, laughter, etc. And physical well-being or illness (Assiah) does give rise to corresponding psychological states. Also, remembering that Yetzirah is the astral level and Assiah the physical, the interface between these two worlds is the etheric plane—the realm of the nature spirits and faerie hosts, and of your own etheric mold.

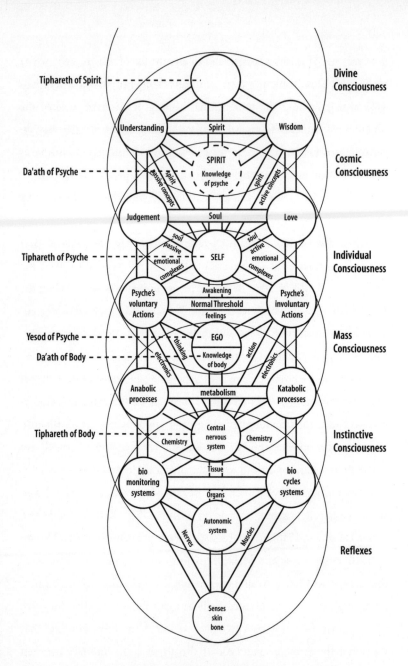

Figure 9. Body and Psyche.
[From *The Work of the Kabbalist* by Z'ev ben Shimon Halevi.

The crown center or chakra is the place where the three lower worlds meet. It is the Kether of Assiah, the crown of the physical body; it is the Tiphareth of Yetzirah, the heart of the psyche, the lower self. Simultaneously, it is the Malkuth of Briah, the opening to the transpersonal higher self or spirit. This shows how the incoming spiritual energy irradiates the psyche and permeates the physical. As a consequence, the astral, etheric, and physical bodies come into alignment and become a clear conduit for the influence from Above.

Figure 9 (see page 114) shows the interpenetration of the physical and the psychological bodies—the microcosmic aspects of the worlds of Assiah and Yetzirah. Study of this diagram will help you begin to understand the way the worlds give rise to and effect one another.

The connection between the psychological and the spiritual is symbolized by the fourteenth tarot key, Temperance. The central figure, Archangel Michael, represents the higher self. One of his feet is on the ground, while the other dips into the waters of the pool. The pool represents Yetzirah, the watery realm of the astral and the psyche. This shows you that the psychological self, although it is the Yetziratic lower self, has access to the higher self that is the regent for the Divine. This connection can manifest through the voice of conscience, in moments of crisis, or in dreams and visions. The golden sky behind the archangel symbolizes Briah, the world of the higher self. The crown in the background represents Atziluth, the native abode of the Divine spark.

The Dweller in Light

Because your lower self has its own agenda to rule everything, much of the early work in the Mysteries is concerned with the regeneration of the personality—literally, to re-generation. The personality is not a fixed, static thing. If it were, there could be no psychological individuation or maturation, no evolution! It is fluid in nature, existing as it does in the watery world of Yetzirah.

All other life forms on our planet are grown and developed by a spiritual intelligence that directs the evolution of each particular species. The feline species is overshadowed by a mighty angelic sometimes called the Great Cat, whose work is to develop the physical species in its charge until it perfectly mirrors the archetype held in Atziluth. This angelic being is the higher self for all cats, from tigers to tabbies, panthers to Burmese. Humankind is different, in that each individual has a distinct higher self, which means that each man and woman will eventually take responsibility for his or her own development, to mirror Adam Qadmon in Assiah, so that God may behold God through human eyes.

Ideally, the personality, the lower self, should be a faithful steward or butler, overseeing the household on behalf of its owner, the spirit, keeping it running smoothly and in right order. However, the personality usurps the place of the owner and uses its not inconsiderable powers to satisfy its own desires, which derive from the vegetable and animal levels of consciousness. Survival, nourishment, shelter, sexuality, social esteem, rivalry, possession, territory, aggression—all these strong appetites derive from the *nephesh,* the vital soul, comprised of vegetable and animal levels. In themselves, they are not intrinsically evil; after all, they are the very impulses that make embodiment possible. We have inherited them from our treading of the way of involution, the veiling of spirit in matter, when we descended from the Divine into physical embodiment. But, once we decide to embark upon the Path of Return, the way of evolution, these impulses must be recognized, purified, and used intelligently to reach our goal, the Beckoning Light. This is why, in some esoteric rituals, humanity is called the Rescuer of Matter.

You have already begun some of the work of regenerating your personality: the building of the subjective Tree of Life, the use of controlled fantasy to image its dynamics and relationships, the circulation of transpersonal power into your subjective spheres, relaxation and discipline. These techniques have all combined to effect a gradual remolding at the subconscious level. But you should not expect your whole psyche to be redeemed just through reading a book. Your regeneration is an ongoing process that extends over preparative stages and admission into the Mysteries. Indeed, many of the workings within the Mysteries are designed to accelerate such a renewal. Every new level of existence you penetrate will require personal adjustment and refinement.

The process is not unlike cleaning a battered and tarnished metal mirror. The mirror is the lower self, the personality or ego. It is dented by the knocks received in your life experience to date, and sooted by the accumulation of false concepts and views that obscure the light of truth. Regeneration is the art and ongoing work of carefully removing the mirror's indentations and polishing its surface with coarse, and then with finer, cloths, until the mirror can reflect detail accurately. This work on your personality is undertaken so that it will become a useful tool in the hands of your higher self, and so clearly reflect the radiance from Above into your physical world, which stands so sorely in need of illumination and grace.

The human soul (as opposed to the vital soul in Yesod) is comprised of the triad of Tiphareth, Geburah, and Chesed. It has the faculties of truth (Tiphareth), discrimination (Geburah), and mercy (Chesed), while the great triad of the spirit is composed of Tiphareth, Binah, and Chokmah. This means that, through Tiphareth, your soul has access to the higher self, your spirit. Your higher self, your spiritual vehicle (sometimes called the mental body), enables you to exist within the flow of time. It contains all the knowledge, experience, and wisdom you have gleaned in all your incarnations.

Contrary to some New Age beliefs, however, the higher self is not perfect; if it were, there would be no need for reincarnation, since its education would be at an end. The vice of hubris is attributed to Tiphareth to emphasize that the higher self is imperfect. Some individuals have incarnated many times and have consequently acquired much experience; they are sometimes called "old souls." Other individuals are fairly recent arrivals, who, being naive, still have much to learn. Some old souls have acquired much experience and power, but, in their pride, seek to manipulate other beings and conditions. The trap of spiritual pride is taught in the allegorical tale of Lucifer. According to tradition, he was the most beautiful of the angels, and God's highest creation before the coming of humanity. Lucifer looked upon his own celestial beauty and power, knew there was no other being like him, and, filled with pride, sought to sit upon the throne of heaven, the seat destined for Adam Qadmon.

Hubris is operative when you consider yourself greater than you are, superior to the masses, and when your will (what you want) appears to you to be the greatest good. Even in your moments of spiritual exaltation, you must beware of gazing upon your own reflection, because your spirit's brightness casts, in Yetzirah, the darkest shadow of all, the cumulative evil of all your incarnations. This accumulation of all your errors is traditionally known as the Dweller on the Threshold. Whenever you see or hear of evils in the world, of appalling crimes and cruelties, before you leap to judge, remind yourself that, in your great journey, there is not one single crime you have not committed yourself. As human beings, we each have the potential to be a Hitler or a Buddha.

Humor

One of the attributes of the higher self that can express itself through the psychological self—at the place where the three lower worlds meet—is humor. By this, I do not mean wit, which is an exercise of the intellect. Nor do I mean the kind of comedy that is based on relief from fear (e.g., the person slipping on the banana skin, who we are delighted is not us). Nor do I mean the experience of physiological joy (playing or exertion) that we share with members of the animal kingdom. Humor, in the sense of the higher self, is the amusement that wells up from the depths of being. It has a transpersonal quality, and usually results from a clear insight into some incongruous aspect of life. It occurs when you are amused by the posturing of your own lower self or the deviousness with which your ego tries to get its own way, or when you realize that you have been replaying the same psychological tape over and over again and your insight and humor disarm it. The humor of your higher self is pure, unbiased, and healing; it redeems your psyche. A good, honest laugh at yourself is more therapeutic than any number of lectures.

In some ways, your lower self is like a child who is upset at not getting its own way. Then down comes the influence of your higher self. It sweeps the child up into its arms, gives it a good-natured hug, and, with its wider vision, imparts to the child a sense of connectedness and well-being. In one of the rituals of ancient Egypt, it was said: "The Priests of Ra purify their hearts with laughter."

Evil, whether objective or subjective, thrives on fear, and it cannot abide laughter that results from genuine humor and realization. Laughter dissolves the hold of evil; it reveals it for the imposter it is. That is why all tyrants fear any laughter except their own, and even that has a hollow ring, for they fear it may echo back on them. Imagine what the consequences would have been if the German nation had laughed at Hitler, had laughed at anyone who held such spiteful and distorted views. Hitler would have been swallowed in obscurity.

The Pattern on the Trestle Board

The Pattern on the Trestle Board is a series of statements numbered from 0 through 10. It was received by Paul Foster Case after asking a Lord of Compassion, the Master Racogsky, to describe his state of awareness

---

0: All the power that ever was or will be is here now.

1: I am a centre of expression for the Primal Will-to-Good which eternally creates and sustains the universe.

2: Through me its unfailing Wisdom takes form in thought and word.

3: Filled with Understanding of its perfect law, I am guided, moment by moment, along the path of liberation.

4: From the exhaustless riches of its Limitless Substance, I draw all things needful, both spiritual and material.

5: I recognize the manifestation of the undeviating Justice in all the circumstances of my life.

6: In all things, great and small, I see the Beauty of the Divine expression.

7: Living from that Will, supported by its unfailing Wisdom and Understanding, mine is the Victorious Life.

8: I look forward with confidence to the perfect realisation of the Eternal Splendour of the Limitless Light.

9: In thought and word and deed, I rest my life, from day to day, upon the sure Foundation of Eternal Being.

10: The Kingdom of Spirit is embodied in my flesh.

Figure 10. The Pattern on the Trestleboard.[11]

when his consciousness was focused within each of the sephiroth (see figure 10, page 120). The number of each statement is related to the appropriate sephira. So, 0 is to Ain, the No-thing; 1 is to Kether; 2 to Chokmah; and so on, through 10, which equates to Malkuth.

The Pattern is a very valuable tool because it helps you relate to the sephiroth through the illumined consciousness of a self-realized person, a Master of Service. Through the telepathic connection that exists subconsciously between all beings, you are able to participate to a degree in this Master's realization of the ten aspects of the One Reality.

THE PATTERN ON THE TRESTLE BOARD

Begin by performing the opening Qabalistic Cross (see page 17) and the relaxation exercise on page 15. Establish the 4:2:4 breathing cycle (see page 16). Build the Middle Pillar in the Queen color scale of Briah, intoning the Divine names. Circulate the white brilliance through your body and aura, both sides, front and back, for at least six complete circuits. Then perform the Fountain Breath Exercise. Continue as follows:

1. Focus on Malkuth on the Tree of your body, and speak its name.

2. Ascend to Yesod and speak its name, then to Hod, saying its name.

3. Continue up the Lightning Flash to Kether, the crown center and the place where the three lower worlds meet. Gently hold your awareness in Kether.

4. Read with awareness The Pattern on the Trestle Board given in figure 10.

5. In numeral order, take each statement from the Trestle Board as your meditation subject for two days. Spend the rest of your meditation session contemplating the statement. Record anything that may occur to you. During the rest of the day, repeat the statement at intervals and note any further insights you may have.

6. Spend two days on each statement—from 0 to 10. For the remaining eight days, focus on any of the statements you found difficult. Often, something you have been studying becomes clearer if you leave it for a while and then return to it.

7. Refocus on Kether, then descend the Lightning Flash, speaking the name of each sephira as you do so. Upon reaching Malkuth, stamp both feet to assert full return to physicality.

Close the session with the Qabalistic Cross and write up your notes in your journal. Once a week, instead of your meditation exercise, I suggest that you do the inner journey visualization in chapter 8.

8

HAIKAL CHOKMAH-NESTORAH: PART 1

Through Wisdom is an house builded:
and by Understanding it is established.

—PROVERBS 24:3

A pathworking is a guided visualization, usually describing an inner journey. The name is derived from the thirty-two paths of the Tree of Life, denoting that you work with the influences of the two sephiroth connected by a path—and it can be hard work!

In this chapter, you will find the first part of a two-part pathworking called the Temple of the Hidden Wisdom (in Hebrew, *Haikal Chokmah-Nestorah*). Part 2 can be found in chapter 12. This journey leads to the great spiritual center, deep upon the inner planes, that stands behind the Qabalistic tradition. The journey enables you to receive the influence flowing through the temple in a controlled and gradated way.

From this point onward, readers who are actually working this book—rather than reading out of interest—are advised to use this pathworking one day a week instead of their usual meditation session. I recommend only doing this pathworking once a week because escapism and astral glamor are powerfully addictive.

You may want to read the pathworking onto a tape recorder, as the journey is detailed and difficult to remember at first. Text ellipses, full-stops, and paragraph breaks should be reflected as pauses in your narration. When recording the pathworking, try to read it as if you are telling an interesting story to a young child. This method of narration is very attractive to the subconscious mind. Since it is the cooperation of your subconscious that you are eliciting, it is important that your style of narration appeal to it.

THE TEMPLE OF THE HIDDEN WISDOM, PART 1

Each time you do the Temple of the Hidden Wisdom exercise, perform an ablution, the Rose-Cross Ritual, and the Interwoven Light Exercises in preparation. Then, in your own words, ask for the Divine blessing upon this interior journey. If no indication is received that the timing is inauspicious, proceed to create the following images. Try to build them vividly and in three dimensions. Endeavor to identify with them by entering into them. You should not simply observe the images as a spectator, but seek to interact with them, to engage them, as the central character.

Before you, there formulates a doorframe fashioned of cedar wood from Lebanon. From its lintel hangs a single violet curtain, embroidered with the glyph of the Tree of Life in silver thread. Focus your attention upon the representation of Da'ath on the curtain's Tree, formulating clearly your intention to journey to the *Haikal Chokmah-Nestorah*. When a breeze springs up from the other side of this doorway causing the curtain to billow, it is a signal that your journey by the inner paths may now begin. Arise from your physical body, leaving it behind, safe within your sacred space, and, drawing back the curtain, step into the mists that lie beyond.

As your vision adjusts to the new level, you begin to see the landscape; you may be surprised to identify it as the location around your physical-plane home. However, the shapes and forms, beings and buildings, have a slightly luminous quality, because you are traveling in the lower face of the Yetzirah, which is the etheric double of the physical world—the "zone girdling the Earth." This is confirmed for you when, passing by gardens and trees in the vicinity, you espy nature spirits vibrating like a drag-onfly's wings and ministering to the various plants and bushes that are their charges. You pass through your neighborhood, from the familiar to the less familiar, until you come to a busy highway. There, you turn your face away from the habitations of men and, walking by the side of the major road, you set out for the countryside.

There is a lot of traffic. The zoom of the cars, the smell of the exhaust emissions, all reflect the preoccupations of the mass of humanity, intent upon their own concerns—security, money, health, happiness—all traveling to and fro, trying to grasp them. The motorway is now passing through the countryside. On the other side, you can see the green of fields that give way to a dis-tant forest. Ahead, a footbridge spans the busy road . . . and by it, you cross over the busy highway of humanity. On the other side, you can walk next to the bushes that fence in the fields. A little way along, you come to a low gate that admits you to a field, beyond which the forest begins. There is an old sign on the gate; it says,

Seeker's Trail. A worn and narrow track leads from the gate, across the field, and into the forest. You climb over the gate . . . through the field . . . and so come to the boundary of the forest.

At the edge of the forest, you nearly stumble across a grass-covered grave. On its small, moss-covered headstone, you can just make out the two words: *A Seeker*. Observe your reactions and the thoughts that arise from the sight of this unknown, hidden tomb. You pass on and into the forest.

The emerald green light from the forest canopy is a contrast to that outside. And so are the inhabitants! For not only is there the flora and fauna of the Earth plane here; the forest also abounds with the denizens of the subtle planes. As you walk the Seeker's Trail, you glimpse, out of the corner of your eye, dryads and elves, the shining ones of the hosts of faerie. But it is amazing just how adaptable the human mind is. For, after walking in this forest a while, you begin to get used to them. And as you peaceably walk, you observe that these beings are similar to humanity, inasmuch as they too have their own preoccupations and labors.

After many hours, you enter a glade comprised of immense trees whose trunks are many arm-spans in width. It is like some vast cathedral of nature, pregnant with the numinous presence of That which lives in all things. By a clear forest pool, you sit down to rest in the tranquil beauty of this place. You fall asleep and dream a dream.

At dawn, you awaken. The first thing you notice is that your attire has changed into a woolen tunic, a hooded, weatherproof cloak, and stout leather sandals. And lying by your side is a pilgrim's staff, a flask of sweet water, and a rolled-up sheepskin. Curious, you unroll the fleece and discover that on the tanned side is painted the Tree of Life. It would seem that you now have a map. You rise, make your ablutions in the forest pool, and continue on your journey.

You think the forest must be coming to an end, because the sunlight is brighter ahead. It continues to increase in strength, more than you are used to. The reason becomes clear when you step from the forest and out onto an immense desert. The golden sands and rolling dunes stretch as far as you can see. Then, a strange grunting sound alerts you . . . you spin around, there is a camel tethered to the last forest tree!

The camel is saddled and harnessed, but examine this "ship of the desert" closely as you approach it, for it is your *nephesh,* your vital soul. It is the instinctual mode of being that you share with all other incarnate life forms. The appearance, the state of health, and the character of this camel will reveal much about your relationship with this aspect of your being. So take a little time now to get acquainted.

That done, you untie the camel and mount up. But which direction to take? You scan the horizon and glimpse something flashing in the distance. Having given your camel a few encouraging prods (stubborn, huh?), you set out across the desert.

You soon get used to the unusual swaying gait of your mount as it treads the sand dunes, rising and dipping like some sea of mineral waves. The flashing you saw has gone, but you persist in the same direction. And your persistence is rewarded when, cresting another dune, you come upon a desert caravan. There are about twenty travelers, all mounted, like you, on camels. You realize the flashing you saw previously was probably sunlight reflecting off the silver bells that adorn the harnesses of the dromedaries.

There is also a group of five men riding horses in the caravan. They appear as medieval knights, armed and wearing chain mail, over which are snow-white mantles adorned with a scarlet emblem of four stylized arrowheads forming an equal-armed cross. These white-cloaked chevaliers seem to be guards, an armed escort.

The leader of the caravan now approaches you. He is dressed for the deep desert and has the Hebrew letter Tau [ת] tattooed on his forehead. He raises the palm of his hand in a gesture of peace; you return his greeting. You explain that you are journeying to the Temple of the Hidden Wisdom and ask for directions. You are delighted when the caravan leader tells that the temple you seek is the destination to which his caravan is traveling. Everyone in the caravan, he explains, is on pilgrimage to the *Haikal Chokmah-Nestorah,* and you are welcome to travel in their company. Gratefully accepting the invitation, you ride to where the leader indicates, falling in beside an elderly man astride a moon-white camel.

The caravan sets off under the strengthening morning sun. All there is to be seen is the undulating golden desert and the azure vault of heaven. It is hot and dry, but the shade of the hood of your cloak gives some respite form the Sun's heat. After a while, the man on the white camel offers you some water from his flask, which you gratefully accept. You introduce yourselves and fall into conversation. There is something familiar about your companion that you can't quite pinpoint. After a few generalities, followed by some gently probing questions, you find yourself relating your life journey to him. And gently, without interrupting, he makes a few comments that reveal how various crises in your life were turning-points, opportunities given by Providence to lead you onto this soul journey.

In such company, the time and distance pass quickly and it is soon noon. The caravan rests in the shade of a few palm trees, sharing water, dates, and rather dry loaves. When the zenith of noon has passed, the leader indicates that it is time to mount up and, escorted by the warrior guardians, the caravan journeys onward.

At one point during the afternoon, you see in the distance an irregular shape that grows larger as the caravan draws nearer. As you approach, you see it is a ruined city. Its walls and buildings have been destroyed by the desert storms; the once proud towers and the domes of temples lay fractured and broken in the dust. The dwellings of the city's rich and poor—its lawgivers and artisans, its merchants and servants—are now home to the lizard and the jackal.

But your soul-sight sees more. Flitting around in the shadows of the shattered masonry, you perceive unclean spirits, like leprous bats, that whisper in the darkness. Intuitively, you know them to be demons, drawn and fed by the evil dreams of the humans living here. Disgusted, you recoil from the sense of corruption still emanating from this once beautiful but wicked city.

"They once thought themselves invincible," your traveling companion comments. "They believed that their city and its increasing wealth was everything. They enslaved the nomads and turned the fertile fields into the desert you now see around you. They thought that their wants justified any action. Finally, their leaders said to Evil, 'Be thou my good'; they turned from the Great Law, and, behold now, the bitter harvest they reaped from that seed of perdition. They are no more; even their name is fallen out of remembrance. And the dwellers of the desert have now renamed this once proud city; they call it *Desolation*.

"What," you ask, "is the Great Law?"

With his eyes fixed upon the far horizon, your companion replies, "That proclaimed by all spiritual masters throughout time: Correct relationship with the source of all life, correct relationship with the rest of life. Let it be known." He falls silent, wrapped in some interior communion. Musing on what has been shown and said, you continue the journey—a journey both in awareness and in understanding.

As the orb of the Sun begins to descend toward the west, the caravan comes to the summit of a particularly high dune and pauses. You sigh when you see the plain below; upon it is a large oasis some five miles across. After the barren monotony of the desert, the verdant green of the trees and the tantalizing glint of sunlight upon water make the oasis appear like paradise.

During the next few hours, the caravan journeys to the oasis. There, tired travelers—humans, camels, and horses alike—are watered. Cooking fires are lit and soon appetizing smells begin to pervade the evening. You join a party engaged in filling the caravan's water-skins for tomorrow's journey.

After a hearty supper and a check on your camel's needs, you spread out your cloak as bed roll, close to that of the man you accompanied during the day. You are strangely drawn to him, because he seems to have answers to many of your questions—and initiates more. You lay down on your back to sleep. Above, through an opening in the canopy of palm branches, you view part of the desert night sky. The stars of the constellation Cygnus, the Swan of Grace, glitter like cosmic diamonds, and you see the blue-white majesty of the planet Jupiter. As you watch, a shooting star arcs across . . . then another . . . then three together . . . then more! Excitedly, you draw your companion's attention to this heavenly display. Smiling he says, "Now relax and view them with soul-sight." So, you lay your head back on the rolled sheep's fleece, raise your consciousness, and focus upon the shooting stars that still speed across the sky. Time slows down, space contracts, so that it seems as if you are in the sky through which living glories speed!

Another shooting star approaches . . . and at the core of its nimbus is a chariot of fire in which rides a Lord of Light, a perfected human spirit. The rider's eyes of sublime radiance pierce you, as the voice fills your mind. "Well met, fellow pilgrim. Like you, we travel to Wisdom's Temple." Then, trailing a blazing arc across the sky, the chariot, the spiritual vehicle of an enlightened being, is gone. Looking up and about, you see that the stars are actually the bodies of mighty archangels, spheres who sing one to another across vast distances, and whose orbits are the creative dance. And for a moment, they are aware of you and their minds brush yours.

Awed, you blink . . . and find yourself back lying on your cloak in the oasis. Around you in the gentle dark come the sounds of gentle snores from the sleepers and an occasional camel grunt. You eyelids close and you dream a dream.

In your dream, you are still within the oasis, but everything seems more ethereal, finer, and more translucent. There is a strong source of light from somewhere deeper within the oasis. You feel drawn to it; you rise and gently drift toward it. It leads you into a little clearing where shines a high column of rainbow light that is centered on a black tent pitched on a small mound. The light is so clear that you can see that the tent has crimson guy-ropes nailed to the ground by gold pegs and that there is a gold trident-shaped ornament crowning the central tent pole. The rainbow light exudes a perfume, like the roses of Damascus.

As you watch, someone emerges from the tent. It is a young, veiled woman. As she walks, the column of rainbow light moves with her, and you realize she is the light's source—or, perhaps, its distillation. Three times this radiant woman circumambulates the little pavilion. Then, before she passes back within, she turns, parts her veil, and looks at you. In that glance, your soul catches fire. Her eyes push you up and beyond form and dream into pure awareness. And as you pass into that abiding, you hear a choral anthem:

O Thou Beautiful! Come upon the winds.
Glide over the waters; sink into my soul.
Then out of the Ocean rose
The Daughter of Light and Fire
The waves were gardens of fragrance.
As the Sun bursts out of a cloud,
As it sheds its glory over the waters:
So from Her morning-eyes
The beauty of love flashed.
Bearer of the Mystic Torch,
Queen of the Choir of the Stars,
Bless me with thy mystic Light.

The light of the dawn upon your eyelids awakens you. Excitedly, you tell your companion about your vision-dream of the fiery chariot and the mysterious rainbow woman.

He nods understandingly, musing half aloud, "Yes, that was She, the bearer of the mystic torch. The embodiment of the

Divine's immanence, whom we call *Kallah,* the Bride, and our Eastern fellow-workers name *Kundalini.* You may yet, God willing, encounter Her again."

Then, surrendering to your infectious enthusiasm, he allows you to pull him along through the oasis, to the little glade of your dream. But upon reaching it . . . you find it's empty! At first, you rush around looking . . . but there is nothing there.

"Calm down," he advises you, "Center down and inhale, smell." You do so . . . and there, there, you can just catch a lingering perfume of the roses of Damascus. "What you experienced is not gone," your companion explains, "just withdrawn from this level." And," he continues, "it is now time for you too, to return to the level from whence you came."

Aghast, you ask, "Do I have to journey all that way back alone?"

Smiling, your companion answers, "No,"as he points across the glade to where now you see the violet curtain embroidered with the silver Tree of Life hanging between the trunks of two palm trees.

"And know too that the caravan and I shall await you here, until you return to us."

A breeze blows in off the desert, causing the veil to billow. Beyond it, you can see your physical sacred space. Thanking your companion deeply, you step through the gate, back into your meditation space, and reseat yourself in the physical chariot of your material body. But before you open your body's eyes and reassert the presence of your consciousness in physicality, inhale once more the perfume of roses.

THE TEMPLE BUILT
WITHOUT HANDS

A saint who thinks he is a saint is no longer a saint.

—TRADITIONAL SUFI SAYING

Looking back over our preceding work, you may be surprised at what you have achieved. If you compare your ability to enter a meditative state of mind now to when you first began, or realize how your skill in visualization has increased, you will see that you have achieved a great deal (more than you may suspect) by undertaking and persevering in self-discipline. You have, in fact, taken responsibility for developing your soul.

The purpose of these exercises has been to instill the fundamental practices necessary for truly esoteric work: relaxation, concentration, visualization, and reflection. These basic skills are the foundation upon which the entire superstructure of the Great Work is built. The temple of the regenerated personality is "built without hands" because it is built by thought alone. Relaxation, concentration, visualization, and reflection are modes of thought. Thought, or will, is consciousness in action.

Thought is the concentration, through one of its individual expressions, of the all-pervading, universal Life-Power. Personality is only a vehicle for that power. The one radiant energy finds expression in all forms. As you read in *The Pattern on the Trestle Board*, "I am a centre of expression for the Primal Will-to-Good, which eternally creates and sustains the universe."

"Be Still, and Know That I Am God"

In previous chapters, you used esoteric techniques (relaxation, breath control, the Middle Pillar, and the Interwoven Light Exercises) to pursue the "science" of meditation. But meditation is also an art. Meditation will serve you as a valid means of development and unfoldment. Regardless of whether you continue with Qabalah or not, the ongoing practice of meditation will enable you to live a fulfilled life—physically, emotionally, and spiritually—because, through the regular practice of meditation, you learn to be responsive to the life-force that nurtures the universe. The benefits of regular meditation are serenity or peace of mind, the awakening of regenerative energies that strengthen your body's immune system and slow the biological aging process, the enlivening of the nervous system, the natural unfoldment of psychic faculties, and the enhancement of creative abilities. Meditation has specific physical results and employs physical energy in the organism of the person engaged in it.

There are different types of meditation. Broadly speaking, they fall into two categories: active meditation and passive meditation. Active meditation utilizes the trained imagination in visualization, the willed construction of images (pathworkings and the like). In passive meditation, on the other hand, you seek identification with the object of meditation. In esoteric practices, both types are used, sometimes in concert. However, these both represent the science of meditation and are transcended by its art. The art of meditation—the skill—is the achievement of a state of pure meditation when consciousness turns in upon itself and abides in a pure, formless state. This is the microcosmic equivalent of *Ain*, No-thing. In Buddhism, this is termed *Shunyata*, and in Hindu yoga, *Brahman*.

Pure meditation transcends the astral and mental levels. It is consciousness being naturally itself. It is being aware of being aware. In tarot, meditation is represented by Key XVII, the Star, but the stillness of the state of pure meditation is imaged by the tarot Key XII, the Hanged Man. He is upside down because meditation reveals the underlying reality behind all appearances, and this brings about a reversal in the day-to-day thinking of the meditator.

Most important illuminations and realizations occur during meditation, when the individual consciousness is immersed in the universal consciousness, when the dewdrop enters the sea. Consequently, meditation is the most important undertaking in your esoteric practice. This is even more true of the practices of a mage or an adept. The main purpose of ceremonials and pathworkings is to introduce images into your subconscious store of pictorial symbols so that, when you receive an illumination from above in meditation, there are suitable images available for your subconscious to clothe it. Once clothed, the illumination can be perceived, retained, examined, and analyzed by your self-conscious mind after you have emerged from meditation.

Meditation is being. All other techniques used in the Mysteries exist only to facilitate this state. Ceremonials are used extensively in training and have an important role in the Magic of Light, but only as a tool. In fact, the most potent and awesome rituals emerge from meditation as visible expressions in Malkuth of what has been 'received upon the Mountain.' But ceremonial for its *own sake* is a detour from attainment—mistaking glamor for the Mystery, the compost heap for the treasure beyond price.

In later work, when you do use ritual, your altar space should be extended into an oratory (a place of prayer). A specific robe will be required. At this point, various rituals of aspiration, purification, and integration become part of your practice. But you should always remember that meditation is the royal road to the crown.

The Seed of the Tree of Life

Your studies and meditations upon the Qabalistic Tree have empowered this great mandala within your consciousness. What follows is a pathworking, an active meditation, whose purpose is to impregnate the seed of the holy Tree of Life into the deeper levels of your subconscious where it can be nourished and grow. The Tree of Life will flourish, putting forth "the leaves that are for the healing of the nations" and bearing the fruit that ripens into the Golden Apples. Use this pathworking as described in the exercise at the end of this chapter.

THE INVOLUTION OF ADAM QADMON

Use the following visualization to plant the seed of the holy Tree of Life. The exercise that follows will help you integrate the visualization into your daily practice.

Close your eyes. You are in darkness. Know yourself to be within Ain-Soph—the boundless, the infinite—and rest, be renewed, within the source of all being. Drift, tranquil and serene, in the nurturing darkness where all things are held in potential. Come now upon a journey with me—a journey beyond time and space, a journey to the beginning of existence. Allow the images described hereafter to form upon the screen of your imagination. Let the "I-Mage" weave its magic.

In the infinity of the No-thing, sense a movement; like a mighty current stirring in the depths, a vast movement that concentrates upon a single point within the heart of infinity. You see a flaring of light, accompanied by a cry that reverberates through all, and a point of white brilliance, like a single star, appears in the velvet darkness.

Something deep within you stirs at the sight of it and you are impelled toward it. You are drawn toward this photon of light. Drawing closer, you see its true magnitude: a vast whirling sphere of incandescence, like burning magnesium, that is pure power. As you approach closer yet, it fills your vision. You are drawn to the orb of white light, backing into it until it surrounds you in its corona. Its dazzling omnipotence shines through you like a prism. You are transfigured into the child of eternity, perfectly at one with Kether, the crown. Feel upon your head the victor's wreath, from which rises the wing feather of the eagle; feel the weight of the staff and wallet upon your right shoulder. You are clothed as a God-in-the-becoming; your inner robe is of the same white brilliance, your outer robe is the mysterious blackness of Ain and ornamented with the ten ineffable lights. You are girded by time itself and, in your right hand, shines the white rose of Divine desire, upon which shines a dewdrop from this primal dawn of a new day of Brahma.

Feel within you the unfettered joy of your God-nature. Know that all obstacles lying before you in the Valley of Manifestation are willed by you! Willed, so that every aspect of your immortal potential may be brought into full actuality. You are an eternal aspect of the Omnipotent; there can be no failure. There will be setbacks and pitfalls upon the Great Journey, each one manifested by you for your delight. But nothing will overcome you, for the All-Power is yours now and always. The greater the obstacle, the greater will be your subsequent victory!

With the blossoming of this knowledge, there arises within you the desire to go forth, to embark upon the Great Adventure. Standing within the primal Sun, you gaze upon the infinite depths. Although invisible, you sense the presence of the ten hidden vessels that await your touch to manifest in existence. Step forth. Light streams forth forming a path beneath your feet. You begin the cosmic dance of the Lightning Flash. As the energy-bliss of your presence passes through the void, the darkness flushes to a deep indigo.

You enter the hidden sphere of the All-Father. As you do, it manifests as a silvery-gray aura about you. The chaiah, the fiery seeds of life, pour into the void as sparkling points of light. You emerge from Chokmah and a radiant path forms beneath the crown so you can traverse to the sephira of the Great Mother.

Entering therein, you see the sphere manifest as a dark iridescence, like a raven's wing, a dark mirror for the Limitless Light beyond. The sound of the waves of a boundless sea is heard. As you come out of Binah, another shining path manifests down and across. You walk down the path to the next veiled sphere.

As you pass into Chesed, there arises from within you a glorious and unqualified compassion that expands all about you as an azure light, blue as a summer's sky. You emerge from Chesed onto the second of the horizontal paths, walking across this bridge of light to the next potential aspect of reality.

You step into the sphere; from within you bursts forth the dynamic strength that creates existence through you. It flares up around you in vivid scarlet, as the strength that achieves all is brought into manifestation. Emerging from Geburah, you walk down a radiant path toward the central axis and enter the hidden heart.

Standing poised within the place of universal balance, you gaze upward, back to the white brilliance from which you emerged. There above you, like a slowly turning galaxy, shines the Sun-behind-the-Sun, abiding and deathless. And below it on either side glows the silver and blue of Chokmah and Chesed, and the indigo and crimson of Binah and Geburah. These five sephiroth hang like great jewels upon the bosom of the Unmanifest. The sight of their glory resonates within you, and, like the phoenix, you give birth to beauty in the sphere of the Sun. Gold light spills from your heart and awakens Tiphareth.

You step from the Sun down a path of light, into a hidden place. Here your pure consciousness undergoes a profound transformation; its crystal clarity is veiled in emotion. Clear awareness of what is becomes clothed within garments of feeling. The variegated spectrum of emotion rises and falls within you, emerging to shine as an emerald glory about you. You walk the last of the horizontal paths from Netzach to hidden splendor.

Within Hod, your consciousness becomes aware of the gymnastics of mentation—forms for abstractions are built, plans laid, concepts investigated, and theories contemplated. You lay claim to the whole diversity of mental and analytic thought, and it shines forth about you as an orange radiance. Walking down toward the Middle Pillar again, you enter the potential foundation of manifestation.

In this sphere, the free-flowing force of the white pillar weaves together with the crystallizing power of the black pillar. Here, the multiplicity inherent in the infinite All becomes actuality. Here life dances in and out of embodiment. The creative process is aroused within you and flares out as irresistible energy, violet, like the gleaming of an amethyst. Emerging from Yesod, you walk the last path into physical manifestation.

At first, there is nothing but mist. But the mists begin to move past your vision. They are clouds veiling the surface of the Earth and, as they part, you can see marvels! You see the Eternal spirit that birthed you standing as mountain ranges; you see spirit shimmering as oceans and seas; you see spirit spread out as fertile fields, vast plains, rippling forests and jungles. Awed, you draw closer into the kingdom. You see the One Life embodied as a fragrant blossom upon an apple tree, and the same One Life in the bee that pollinates it. You feel the One Life leap as a silver salmon from Itself flowing as a river. You view the Eternal One as thousands of buffalo stampeding across a sea of grass, and in a million industrious ants about their nest. You hear it trilling through the birds of the air, howling at dusk as the wolves of the tundra, singing mysteries in the blue depths as whale song. Everywhere you look, the One Spirit of Life stands, sits, runs, leaps, flies, sings, loves, births, dies, and continues to *be*. It was for this that the Most Holy One willed existence into being; all the preceding sephiroth on the Tree of Life find their justification in Malkuth.

And what of splendid, ignorant, noble, cruel, and sad humanity? What is its place in *Kallah*, the Bride that is Malkuth? Humanity, in all its diversity and with all its growing pains, *is the same as you:* a message of love from God to the Earth, and a prayer from the Earth back to God.

And when you have traversed the Lightning Flash back up to the source, the dance will be completed . . . and God shall be all in all.

PLANTING THE SEED OF THE HOLY TREE

Begin by performing the opening Qabalistic Cross (See page 17) and the relaxation exercise on page 15. Establish the 4:2:4 breathing cycle as described on page 16. Build the Middle Pillar in the Queen color scale (see page 49), intoning the Divine names, and perform the Fountain Breath Exercise for at least six cycles (see page 99).

1. Ascend the Tree of the body by the Lightning Flash, speaking the name of the sephiroth as you focus on each sphere. When you have reached Kether, check that you are still physically relaxed.

2. For one session in each week, work the pathworking The Involution of Adam Qadmon (see above).

3 For the other four sessions in the week, after you have ascended the Tree of the body to Kether, use the most high and

holy name of the Ineffable One as a mantra: *I am that I am*. As you do so, focus on Kether for the first *I am*, then on Malkuth for *that*, and back to Kether for the second *I am*.

4. Keep on gently repeating this mantra with awareness of who is being aware of whom. Allow this mantra to help you gently shift consciousness. When it feels right, cease the repetition and just *be*.

When you emerge from your meditative state, repeat the Fountain Breath Exercise for another six cycles. Seal your aura with the closing Qabalistic Cross, have a good stretch, then write up your notes in your journal.

10

THE TETRAGRAMMATON

A poor devotee points to the sky and says,
"God is up there."
An average devotee says, "God dwells in the heart
as the Inner Master."
The best devotee says, "God alone is, and everything I perceive
is a form of God."

—RAMAKRISHNA

FROM *THE WISDOM OF THE HINDU GURUS*

The word *Tetragrammaton* means: "the name of four letters." The four Hebrew letters of this name are: Yod, Heh, Vau, Heh, usually pronounced Yahveh and, in Latin, Jehovah. This sacred name means "That which was, That which is, and That which will be"—in other words, the Eternal, the One Reality, which alone is changeless and is the causeless cause of existence. Each of the four letters is assigned to one of the four Qabalistic worlds, and to one of the sephiroth: Yod to Atziluth and the sephira Chokmah, the first Heh to Briah and the sphere of Binah, Vau to Yetzirah and to Tiphareth, and the final Heh to Assiah and

Malkuth. What is being represented to us here is the vertical unfoldment from Above to Below, the One Life expressing itself through all the descending orders of creation, and the veiling of itself in all forms. As the individual letters can only form a word or name when they are joined together, so too the Four Worlds and all they contain need to be read as one thing, as a unity, if we are to understand the purpose of existence and our place within it.

This fourfold division is reflected in each sephira of the Middle Pillar of the Tree of Life. In Kether, this quaternary is expressed as the *Chaioth-ha-Qodesh*, the four holy living creatures—the winged human, the winged lion, the winged ox, and the eagle. These angels of Kether are depicted at the corners of tarot Keys X and XXI, the Wheel and the World. From these holy creatures flows the fiery sweat, the grace that upholds and nourishes the Four Worlds.

In Da'ath, the quaternary is expressed through the four archangels of the presence: Raphael, Michael, Gabriel, and Auriel. Their names are codes for the Divine attributes of healing, perfection, strength, and enlightenment.

In the sixth sephira, Tiphareth, the quaternary are the four supervisors of the elemental hosts, traditionally called kings. They are Paralda, Djinn, Nixsa, and Ghob. Because these four elemental kings appear as their subject-charges, many seers have mistaken them for being of the same order of creation as those they oversee. But Paralda appears as a celestial super-sylph (air spirit) to relate to his charges, the sylphs of air, in the same way that many people still think of deity as a "big human." The four elemental kings are not of the elemental order at all. They belong to the choir of the *Malakhim* of Tiphareth; they are angels of the Sun.

In Yesod, the ninth sephira on the Tree, the quaternary is expressed through the four elemental orders: the sylphs of air, the salamanders of fire, the undines of water, and the gnomes of earth. These names and classifications were first given in the West by Paracelsus, who drew them from classical sources: sylph from *sipha* (meaning "butterfly"), salamander from *salambe* (meaning "fireplace"), undine from *unda* (meaning "wave"), and gnome from *ge-nomos* (meaning "Earth dweller").

Elemental spirits live in the etheric interface between the worlds of Assiah and Yetzirah, the zone between the physical and astral levels. Elementals, as they are often called, are units of living consciousness that permeate the so-called inanimate forms of matter.

The key to understanding what, in the Mysteries, is meant by the terms air, fire, water, and earth lies in knowing that these are not references to physical air, fire, water, or earth at all. This is why they are properly termed air of the wise, fire of the wise, etc. A ceremonial invocation of fire does not summon physical fire (if it did, the participants would be incinerated); it is an invocation of the One Energy in its radiant aspect. An invocation of water calls upon the One Energy in its fluid aspects. Invocations to air and earth call upon it in its gaseous and solid or inert aspects respectively (matter being frozen energy). This One Energy is the root substance of all that is; for this reason, alchemists name it both First Matter and the Quintessence. The elements are four aspects of the One Life-Force, in the same way that the four letters comprise one name. Gas, radiance, liquid, and solid are the primal patterns made and composed of the all-pervading energy in order to produce everything that we see, hear, taste, smell, and touch. The One Thing is the mental substance of the all-pervading consciousness, the mind of God.

In the tenth and final sephira, Malkuth, the fourfold activity of the One Energy is symbolized by the four fixed signs of the zodiac: Aquarius for air, Leo for fire, Scorpio for water, and Taurus for earth. Aquarius is the winged human. Scorpio's force, when sublimated, becomes the eagle of aspiration. So we see, veiled in Malkuth, the same four holy creatures who are the angels of Kether. This is one meaning of the Qabalistic aphorism: Kether is in Malkuth, and Malkuth is in Kether.

The Magic Circle

As the number zero, the circle is the mathematical symbol of Ain, the No-thing, the Absolute. The all-embracing circle is a symbol of all that is, the serpent swallowing its own tail. Objectively, the circle represents the Macrocosm; subjectively, it represents the Microcosm, the individual's sphere of sensation or aura. When you stand in the magic circle, you are the axis about which the universe revolves. The seven mystical directions encompass the circle—Above and Below, the four cardinal points, and the center, which is the "Palace of Holiness in the midst, sustaining all things."

In the ritual aspect of the Work, the cardinal points of east, south, west, and north are defined by gateways, watchtowers, or portals. These three terms refer simply to a point through which energy may flow either into or out of the magic circle. When a circle has no gateways formed in its circumference, it is called a *circle of safety*, and is used for defense work and for evocation from the depths. Few practitioners know there is a fifth portal at the center of the circle, the *portal of spirit*. This gate of the Quintessence joins Above with Below, east with west, and north with south. In most ceremonies, the altar standing at the center functions as this portal.

The Portal of the East

The east is associated primarily with the spiritual light to which we aspire and the resultant wisdom of illumination, since this is the direction of the Sun arising each morning. Most ceremonial workings of the Mysteries are oriented (as the word implies) toward the east. When you look at a tarot key, in most cases, you are looking toward the east, so what is on the right-hand side of the card is south, the foreground west, and the left-hand side north. In the Tree of Life diagram the same is true: on a horizontal axis, Kether is the east and Malkuth the west.

Attributions of the eastern gate are: wisdom, dawn, Archangel Raphael, Paralda, the sylphs, air, spring, the Vernal Equinox, the sign of Aquarius (fixed air), the spiritual core of your being, birth, the beginning of any new cycle.

The Portal of the South

The spiritual principle of love is attributed here. The Solar Logos, as the transmitter of all energy to this solar system, transmits all the ranges or frequencies of the universal radiant energy. Some of these can be measured by scientific instruments; others are as yet beyond measurement. What science calls gravity is the same force that the ageless wisdom calls love. This will repay meditation.

Attributions of the southern gate are: love, noonday, Archangel Michael, Djinn, the salamanders, fire, summer, the Summer Solstice, the sign of Leo (fixed fire), youth, waxing in strength.

The Portal of the West

The spiritual principle of power (or life) is attributed to the west. This refers particularly to the etheric level that sustains physicality. It is the ebbing and flowing of the etheric tides that cause the growth and decay of all embodied forms.

Attributions of the western gate are: life, dusk, Archangel Gabriel, Nixsa, the undines, water, autumn, the Autumnal Equinox, the sign of

Scorpio (fixed water), maturity, full physical expression, the resultant appearance of any inner causation.

The Portal of the North

The spiritual principle of law is assigned the northern quarter. This refers to universal law, not to the shifting *mores* of human societies. Divine law is constant throughout all cycles of expression, and to those who learn those laws and live accordingly, the law becomes the "sure foundation that changeth not." This is one meaning of the parable told by Jesus about the house (your house of life) built upon the rock rather than on shifting sand.

Attributions of the northern gate are: law; Archangel Auriel, Ghob, the gnomes, earth, winter, the Winter Solstice, the sign of Taurus (fixed Earth), death, transformation, and alchemy.

The Quintessence

At the circle's center is the gate of spirit, corresponding to the Quintessence. In the Eastern Mystery teachings, the Quintessence is called *Akasha,* which means the "mixing bowl of the elements." The center is the fourth dimension, which transcends space—three-dimensional consciousness. It is eternity, which transcends time. In old esoteric texts, the Quintessence was referred to by the technical term *Azoth*. This artificial word is comprised of the first and last letters of the Latin, Greek, and Hebrew alphabets—in Latin, A and Z, in Greek, Alpha (A) and Omega (O), and in Hebrew, Aleph (A) and Tau (Th). What is intimated here is that, in spirit, beginning and ending are one. Never has there been a time when spirit was not. In all places and times, spirit is. And at the end of any cycles, whether vast or minute, there remains spirit without diminishment. This fifth portal is used in invocation from the heights.

The Perpetual Light

Earlier, you set up an altar before which you performed your meditations and upon which you placed a lamp or candle to represent the Divine presence. Now you are going to extend your private meditation area into a sanctuary, a sacred place, an oratory.

The ceremonial lamp is called the perpetual light because it symbolizes the Divine presence that forever shines in the heart (center) of every human being. It is sometimes called the Inner Light, which is also a title of Kether; Christian mystics refer to it as the light of Christ; in Hindu metaphysics, it is called the *atman*, and in Qabalah, it is called *ruach*. Do not think that this is just poetic imagery; it is a real fact that can be seen and experienced. In the subtle or etheric body, the heart chakra receives the universally diffused radiant energy and concentrates it. This inner light, the core of your being, is the cause of your sense of individuality, your "I-ness." But it is not, and never can be, separated from the its source, the Limitless Light. It is a concentration of the Divine light, but not separate from it. All ceremonial actions, such as saluting or bowing in reverence to the physical light upon a ceremonial altar, are reminders of this indwelling light. An accurate translation of the Greek version of St. John's gospel is: "This is the true Light that lighteth every man coming into the world . . . and the Word was made flesh, and dwelt within us."[12] Whenever you sit before the perpetual light burning on your altar, you should be aware that it is all part of the single living flame—the fire of life—that has its originating spark in the heart of God. It is a well-attested fact that, when advanced yogis and adepts die (medical death), their vacated physical bodies show no sign of decomposition or decay for at least three days. The body retains its upright posture and the skin remains supple. *Rigor mortis* is not present, but a warmth is detectable in the region of the heart. When this warmth ceases, the vacated body collapses and the usual signs of death appear.

From now on, before any meditation sessions or ritual working, your very first act should be the lighting of the lamp. You may use a match or lighter; a taper is best. This may seem so simple, yet this one act has resonances and realizations of the primal act of creation—the original *Fiat lux*, "Let there be light." After all, this is what true magic is all about . . . re-creation. The lighting of the lamp of the Divine presence is a moment of supreme affirmation performed with spiritual intention that you are expressing the Divine within your sacred space, your environment, indeed within your whole sphere of influence. Your whole aura will light up, and the more vibrant and brighter your aura becomes, the greater and more potent your powers for good will be. This *is* L.V.X., the light in extension.

You should bring all this to mind as you light the match or taper and hold it up at arm's length over the lamp, saying, *From Thee, O Effulgent One, comes all Grace*. Then light the lamp and gaze at its radiance, declaring: *Behold, the Light shineth in darkness, and the darkness cannot overcome it*. Now you can proceed with your meditation or ceremony.

The Rainbow Gate

Portals, doors, or gateways are images used to enter and exit the inner levels. They allow you to travel safely to the upper worlds or, as they are also called, the inner planes. They are established as objective doorways by inner-plane intelligences and initiated adepts and are strengthened by the use of generations of initiates and accepted students. An experienced mage will use many gateways to many different locations: various temples of the spirit, halls of initiation, places of healing, physical locations, and alternative realities. Advanced adepts may perform "gating," the willed creation of temporary portals fashioned by pure energy.

The fundamental rule of portals is simple and must be adhered to if you intend to "walk the worlds" safely. Whatever gateway is used to pass out into the unseen must also be used to return to physical consciousness. Failure to do so, in the early stages, can lead to psychological disassociation; in advanced training, it can lead to falling between the worlds, resulting in physical coma and/or death. By imparting this teaching, understand that I am clearly stating that I take no responsibility for any reader who decides to ignore this safeguard.

You are already familiar with one such inner doorway, the one in the *Haikal Chokmah-Nestorah* meditation in chapter 8. You will now be introduced to another ancient and potent portal. This portal is a very rare exception, however, in that it can be used to pass through before sleep; your soul will naturally return through it subconsciously as you awaken. But I reiterate that this Rainbow Gate is an exception to the rule. There are no attendant dangers to using it because it was designed for such a purpose. This particular portal leads to one of the great teaching centers on the inner planes. For over a millennium, some of the greatest master-teachers of the Mysteries taught in the temples, porticoes, and colleges of this center of ageless wisdom. And upon the inner levels, they still teach their pupils and many an aspiring soul, brought there for instruction while the physical body sleeps.

THE RAINBOW GATE EXERCISE

In appearance, the Rainbow Gate is a pylon gate fashioned of white stone and carved with many ancient symbols. The winged

Sun-disc, fashioned in gold, shines upon the lintel, from which hangs, between the uprights, a rainbow-colored veil.

To use this gate, first perform the Evening Review (see page 29) and compose yourself for sleep. Then build up the image of the Rainbow Gate. When it is clear, step through the rainbow veil. You will find yourself in a vast park. There are beautiful trees and shrubs, fountains and pools. Splendid buildings are dotted about the park. This place represents one of the greatest flowerings in human history, all dedicated to the attainment of wisdom. You may wander through these gardens, but not enter any of the buildings. You will find pleasant little groves in the park, shady trees and cool marble benches. Make yourself comfortable and wait for sleep to come here, one level removed from the physical plane. In dreams, One may come and guide you.

At first it is not advisable to use this portal more than twice a week. Always make sure that you record any dreams you have when you have used this gateway. Include them in your journal.

QUARTERING THE CIRCLE EXERCISE

Place your altar in the center of your meditation area, so that you can walk around it. If this is not possible, then perform the following steps in your imagination. Your colored Tree of Life diagram should be on the eastern wall. After your ablution, enter your sacred space and commence by performing the lighting of the perpetual light (see page 151). Then perform the Qabalistic Cross. Sitting in the west, facing east, relax and begin the 4:2:4 breathing cycle (see page 16). Build up the Middle Pillar in full color (see page 49), perform the Fountain Breath Exercise at least six times, then image the spiraling light clockwise from Malkuth into Kether.

1. Consider the four quarters of the universe, what you have learned about them in this chapter and elsewhere.

2. Select a quarter, then, with intention stand and go to it; making sure you always walk in a clockwise direction around the altar.

3. Standing before the quarter, build up the image of an open door, through which you can see a landscape that is evocative of the attributions of that quarter. For example, if you chose the west, fantasize a seashore at dusk.

The Sun has just set; the first stars are appearing, and there is a crisp autumnal wind whipping the waves. Then . . . the Moon, the Queen of Heaven, rises up out of the waters. The moonlight makes a silver pathway on the sea that leads up to the open door. As you watch in the enchanted light, you begin to see beautiful forms cavorting among the waves—mermaids and tritons, the undines frolicking in the sea. Then, rising from the deep, comes a great chariot made from a single shell and pulled by seahorses, white as foam. In the chariot rides Nixsa, King of the Undines. He wears the form of some ancient sea god.

Really put yourself into the scene; see it, feel it, taste the salt-laden wind upon your tongue.

4. Then picture the door closing and a bar coming down across the door, keeping it safely closed by your will.

5. Spend one week's work (five days) on each quarter. Working with all four quarters will complete this chapter's work.

You may want to make or obtain a robe, or, if appropriate, a *tallit*, a prayer shawl. You can use this in your future rituals and meditations, wearing it in the presence of sacred powers and spiritual intelligences. Make sure, however, that it is worthy of them and of you.

11

STAR OF THE MAGI

Mystery is to God what privacy is to Man

—APHORISM

A symbol—from the Greek word *simbuon*, meaning "thrown together"—is a representation of an unseen force, concept, or idea. In magical practice, a symbol representing a force is called a *sign of power*. This is an artificial symbol, usually built up by thousands of years of use, associating it in the collective unconscious of humanity with that which the symbol represents. Tarot is a composition of such symbols, skillfully assembled to form the various tableaux of the Major Arcana. As such, tarot speaks in the universal language of symbol and picture. This is the language of the subconscious. In a previous chapter, we studied and worked with the great Tiphareth symbol of the Rose-Cross. In this chapter, we will study and practice the arcane symbol of the five-pointed star, the sacred pentagram.

The Complementaries

Of the three pillars on the Tree of Life, the two outer pillars—The Pillar of Mercy (Chokmah, Chesed, and Netzach), and the Pillar of Severity (Binah, Geburah, and Hod)—are called the Complementaries, because they complement one another. The Pillar of Mercy is the Yang of Taoist philosophy, and the Pillar of Severity the Yin. Kether, therefore, is the Tao. The white Pillar of Mercy is expansive, the life-giving-force aspect of the One, while the black Pillar of Severity is contraction, the embodying-form aspect of the One. In the Temple of Solomon (and in the lodges of Freemasonry), these two pillars are named *Jachin* (mercy) and *Boaz* (severity). They are shown as such in tarot Key II the High Priestess. The white column bears the Hebrew Yod and the black column the letter Beth; hanging between them is a woven veil showing ten pomegranates arranged as the ten fruits of the Tree of Life. All of creation is woven like a tapestry upon the frame of energy and structure. This is symbolized by the floor design of the temple: alternating black and white squares.

In the last exercise, you meditated on the gates of the elements, placed at the quarters of the circle. These elements are the four modes by which the One Radiant Substance manifests: gaseousness, radiance, fluidity, and solidity. These elements of the wise relate also to the twin pillars of the Complementaries. Fire is unconditioned force; water is unconditioned form; air is conditioned force, and earth is conditioned form.

The Middle Pillar of the Tree of Life (Kether, Tiphareth, Yesod, and Malkuth) is the pivot of balance between the Complementaries of force and form, and is therefore also the point of control. The Middle Pillar, you will recall, is the Pillar of Consciousness and Grace. In the Western esoteric tradition, the candidate for initiation receives the seed of light (grace) while in a heightened state of consciousness, while between the pillars of night and day.

When teaching about the Rose-Cross ceremony, I made several references to the Banishing Pentagram ritual. In essence, the Banishing Pentagram ritual is used to scrub clean the place or person who performs it of all extraneous influences. The ritual can be used to invoke, evoke, or banish entities, to dissolve thought-forms, and to subjugate undesirable forces or beings.

Now this is a big claim. What is its justification? Unless we intend to be sorcerers, operating out of superstition, working on the lower astral level alone, we are going to have to do better than this. In fact, if you have no true knowledge of what the pentagram symbolizes, what it actually "says" to inner-plane beings through communication by symbols, the rite will be ineffectual. The ignorant fringe of occultism is full of people who load themselves down with cheap silver jewelry shaped like pentagrams. They draw this symbol at any ordinary shadow or unpleasant truth that comes near them. The only thing that saves them from serious damage is their ignorance. Their shadows are usually projections of their own psyches, and the symbol they draw is empty of any real meaning or power. A mage is one who understands each and every symbol he or she employs—an understanding born of realization and knowledge, realization that is the fruit of meditation, knowledge that is transmitted by the lineage of initiated teachers.

Gematria

In the literal Qabalah, we use *Gematria*, the science of interpreting the esoteric teachings veiled in the scriptures. The Rabbis said, "The man who interprets the Scriptures literally is a fool." Gematria is used to reveal the wisdom concealed in the Bible, which is the Wisdom Book of the Western esoteric tradition. Thus, Gematria is the Western form of

Gnana Yoga, a "union by means of knowledge." Simply put, Gematria is the contemplative study of words that have the same numerical values, so giving new emphasis to one another for the purpose of occult reconciliation, which results in the transcendence of opposites. For, when wisely used, Gematria leads your thoughts, step by step, away from outer forms to interior meanings. It is a method for gaining firsthand knowledge of the truths concealed in Hebrew, Greek, and Latin words and other Mystery phrases through instruction from within. This, when wedded to mystical realization, establishes, within your consciousness, a foundation upon which can be built an abiding awareness of the Primordial Unity that lies at the heart of creation.

Each letter of the Hebrew alphabet is also a number. (This is true of the Greek and Latin alphabets as well.) Aleph = 1; Beth = 2; Mem = 40; Resh = 200; etc. Words having the same numerical value reveal hidden teachings, veiled from the profane. However, to benefit from this truly magical language, the Qabalist must be thoroughly grounded in the principles of the secret wisdom. Gematria is a practice that must be used with caution, as occult history shows many cases of stupidity, ego-inflation, or dry intellectualism resulting from its misuse. Most teachers agree that Gematria is best reserved for students at the Journeyman level (one thoroughly versed in the tradition and studying under a Craftsman).

But when the cat is out of the bag, one cannot ignore it. So, as a rule of thumb, the use of Gematria is only applied to names of persons or places (e.g., Abel, or Jerusalem), to measurements (Noah's ark, Solomon's Temple, the Heavenly City) given in the scriptures, and to the angles of measurement in sacred Geometry, which go back to the priesthoods of Egypt and Chaldea. In the following teaching, we will use it to analyze the pentagram.

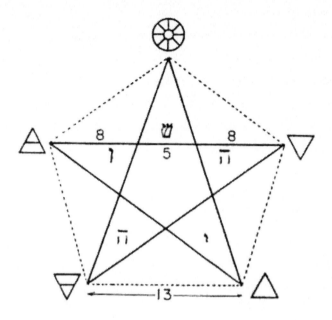

Figure 11. The Pentagram.

The numbers of the pentagram are part of sacred Geometry used in the Pythagorean School of the Soul in Krotona. Pythagoras learned it from the hierophants of Egypt. This is called the Golden Section. Just as certain words are codes for universal laws and operations, so the relationships in certain numerical sequences conceal and reveal (to those who have been instructed) sacred relationships in the Macrocosm and, therefore, by inference, in the Microcosm.

In figure 11 above, the bottom line of the pentagon that surrounds the pentagram has the number 13. The upper horizontal line has the numbers 8, 5, and 8. These digits correspond most nearly to the actual subdivision of this line into extreme and mean proportion. That is to say, 5 (the length of the short segment of the line) is approximately to 8 (the length of the long segment of the line) as 8 is to 13 (8 + 5 = 13). Likewise, 8 is to 13 approximately as 13 is to 21 (the length of the whole line, 8 + 5 + 8 = 21). These numbers give valuable Qabalistic insights into the deep symbolism of the pentagram.

When a pentagram is traced in the air with a sword or other magical implement, the enclosing pentagon is defined, but not actually described. For this reason, the pentagon is usually shown by dotted lines. Since each line of the enclosing pentagon is 13, the sum of all five sides is 65, the numeric value of *Adonai*, "My Lord," the special Divine name for Malkuth.

Sixty-five is also the number of the noun *haikal*, meaning "temple" or "palace," and of the verb *haws*, meaning "hush, keep silence." So we read in Habbakuk 2:20, "The Lord is in His holy temple, let all the earth keep silence before Him."

The occult meaning of this is that all the activities of a human being (symbolized by the pentagram, as shown in Leonardo da Vinci's engraving of a man with arms and legs outstretched in its shape) are carried on *within* the being of Adonai, the Lord: "In Him we live and move and have our being." Nothing done by any human being is separable from the sum total of the Life Power's expression. The five interwoven lines of the pentagram star represent the web of life in which all beings live and interact with one another—from the highest expressions to the most basic.

In alchemy, each of the four elements is symbolized by a triangle. These triangles form the points of the pentagram symbol. The clear upright triangle is fire, an upright flame (bottom right); the clear down-pointing triangle is the cup of water (upper right); the upright triangle with a bar across it is for air, a mountain with a cloud across its peak (upper left); and the down-pointing triangle with a bar across it is for earth, a nail driven into the ground (bottom left). The symbol at the fifth point—an eight-spoked wheel—is the alchemical symbol of the Quintessence, the First Matter. This symbol is shown embroidered upon the doublet worn by the Fool in tarot Key 0. It is of interest that, in the older tarot decks, this key was called The Alchemist. By this detail, the four expressions of the life-power—the elements of the wise you studied in the previous chapter—are shown to be the interacting tools whereby the One Spirit (the Quintessence) manifests itself in an infinite array of forms.

Each of the five lines of the pentagram is 21 units long. This number is the value of the Divine name *Eheieh*, "I Am," assigned to Kether, the crown. This is the self-declaration of the Absolute that is the One Reality. In Qabalistic psychology, this is *Yekhidah*, the unique and indivisible part of us often called the Divine spark. It thus becomes plain that, when a pentagram is traced in ceremonial magic, each of its five lines stands for Eheieh, so that the figure declares to all beings who behold it that humanity is not only surrounded and conditioned by the being of the Absolute, but also is a special manifestation of the spiritual power proceeding from Yekhidah in Kether. Consequently, in using the pentagram ceremonially, an instructed Qabalist will, by gesture and visualization, impress the subconscious mind with the most powerful suggestions. Nature is the lesser part, a human is the greater part, and God is the whole.

To the uninstructed, nature appears to be greater in extent and in mass, but the teaching of the sages affirms that the true measure is not in terms of size but in terms of consciousness. The universe is mental, and humanity's mental capacity is greater that that of nature. Humanity is to nature as God is to humanity. An alchemical axiom says: Nature unaided always fails. This, however, does not mean that humanity should abuse nature, but rather that we should exercise wise and insightful stewardship and, more, that, by our evolving consciousness, we should bring about that state of being, in full physicality, symbolized by such images as the Garden of Eden or the Heavenly Jerusalem brought to Earth.

The Messiah

Because the number 21 is the sum of the numbers from 0 to 6 inclusive (called the "Theosophic extension" of 6), it relates to Tiphareth. Each line of the pentagram represents an extension, or full expression, of the power of the sphere of the Sun. As you know, the higher self (or Holy Guardian Angel) is assigned to Tiphareth. It is an individualized aspect of the collective of Tiphareth. This collective, in its totality, is Tiphareth; in Rosicrucian symbolism, this is the Christ. Now here, we are not teaching any dogmatic or theological concepts of Christ; we are referring to the universal power of redemption, reconciliation, and balance.

Esoterically, it is taught that the Christ (the Anointed One) is an office, like that of a president or the master of a Freemasonic lodge. This office is held by different individuals at different times. It is taught that there is always a man or woman upon this planet who, for their time, fills that office as the Axis of the World, upon whom all grace rests. The Christ is head of the incarnate hierarchy. To use Rosicrucian terminology, the holder of the sublime office of the "Anointed of their time" is the *Ipsissimus* who has attained the perfect realization of the Kether of Assiah: "I and my Father are One." There are ten such incarnate Ipsissimi, each one holding the perfect realization of Kether, in each of the sephiroth of the world of action—Assiah. For, remember, there is a Tree within each sephira. These ten constitute the senior three tiers of the incarnate hierarchy: the One [the Christos], the Three, and the Six.

But when we talk of Tiphareth as the spiritual collective of human-ity, we are speaking of the Christ force, the universal power of at-one-ment. "The Christ within" is a term used by some Rosicrucian Qabalists to distinguish between the Divine within a human being and the Divine transcendence, between the immanence in the heart-of-hearts and the ineffable Absolute. This is the same as the Buddha nature inherent in all beings taught by the lamas and yogis.

In the Greater Mysteries, the pentagram is often refereed to as the Star of Christ. Within each of the five points is a Hebrew letter. These are the four letters of the Tetragrammaton, *Yod-Heh-Vav-Heh*, and the holy letter *Shin*. Shin is placed between the two first and last letters, so read-ing: *Yod-Heh-Shin-Vav-Heh*, spelling the name *Yeheshua*. This is a rendi-tion of the Hebrew name Joshua, the successor of Moses. It is also the name of the man commonly called, by the Latin translation, Jesus. Joshua means "Yah liberates." What is intimated here is that it is the nature of the One Reality *(Yod-Heh-Vav-Heh)* to overcome all limita-tions. It also intimates that the human desire for liberty originates in the superconscious levels and has a spiritual impulse. The holy letter Shin, placed in the middle of the four letters of the Tetragrammaton, indicates that God, the One Reality, ensouls the human temple, that he is the true dweller in the heart.

In Qabalah, this Cosmic Christ, or Tiphareth, of which all men and women are spiritually a part (consciously or unconsciously) has three names. The first is *Melekh*, "the King," and thus the principle of rulership. Tiphareth is the active manifestation of that principle, the ruler who wears the crown (Kether). The second title of Tiphareth is *Ben*, "the Son." Here, don't think in terms of persons; think rather of a smaller expression of the One. Remember, Tiphareth heads the lesser counte-nance (see page 42). The sephira of Tiphareth has paths that connect it with Binah, the Great Mother, and with Chokmah, the All-Father. So it is the "son" of these supernal parents.

The third name is *Adam*; it is regarded in the secret teachings as the generic term for *all* humanity. The Hebrew noun *Ish* is used for individual humans, or for humans as they are now. This may sound confusing until you remember that the Adam referred to here is none other than Adam Qadmon.

You must always remember, in your study of the Tree of Life, that you are dealing with a single power as it presents itself to the human mind. The sephiroth are not ten things, but ten expressions of One Power. It is your mind that creates the illusion of separateness, of being apart. Yet your mind is capable of receiving the corrective and illuminating influence from superconscious levels that enable you to transcend the dualistic activity of intellect and so to realize the real unity hidden under the appearance of the many.

When you as an instructed practitioner ceremonially draw the pentagram, you are asserting, in gesture, the proportionate relationship between God and humanity, and between humanity and nature. You thus remind yourself—and all other beings—that the actions you perform are part of the Divine order, and so affirm that what you say or do is done by one who knows their self to be *zel-Shaddai,* an image of the Almighty One.

Woven Paces and Waving Hands

The symbol of the pentagram has twelve ways of being drawn with ritual intention: an invoking and a banishing tracing for each of the four elements, and tracings for spirit in both its active and passive modes. These twelve pentagrams make up the Crown of Twelve Stars that surrounds the head of the Shekinah. For the purposes of this chapter, we will focus on the most commonly used, the Banishing Pentagram of Earth. The following is from Dion Fortune's book, *Psychic Self-Defense*:

In dealing with Elementals or non-human entities, the Pentagram, or Pentalpha, is the best weapon. This is the five-pointed star drawn in a particular way. Pointing the first and second fingers of the right hand [left if you are left-handed], and folding the others into the palm and touching their tips with the thumb, proceed to draw the Pentagram in the air, keeping the elbow stiff and swinging the arm at full length. Start with the right arm across the body, the hand at about the level of the left hip [This corresponds to the bottom left angle of the pentagram in the diagram, the one indicated by the barred, down-pointing triangle of earth.], the extended fingers pointing downwards and outwards. Swing it upwards, as if drawing a straight line in the air until the fingers point straight above the head at arm's length [Quintessence symbol]. Now sweep it down again, keeping the elbow stiff, until the hand occupies the corresponding position on the right side [angle marked by fire symbol] to that which started on the left. You have now drawn a gigantic "V" upside down. Next swing the hand across the body, on a rising incline, until it is stretched on a level with the left shoulder [angle marked by air symbol]. Bring it across the body horizontally until it is in the same position to the right [water], fingers pointing away from the body. Now swing it downwards across the body till the hand has come back to the point by the left hip whence it started. This is an exceptionally potent sign. The value of the Five-pointed Star, the symbol of Humanity, is widely

167

known among occultists, but its potency depends upon the manner in which it is drawn. The method I have given is the correct one for banishing.[13]

This is the Banishing Pentagram of Earth. Notice there is no repeating of the first line as some Wiccan groups teach (to prevent the power leaking out!). That would render the symbolism of this sign of power null and void. What Dion Fortune omits to mention is that, upon completing the pentagram, you place your hand in the center of the star with a stabbing gesture and speak the Divine name of power appropriate to the working. This, in effect, charges the sign with power, and "lights it up."

The purpose of the Banishing Ritual of the Pentagram is to purify a place of all influences. Its successful performance removes all emotional charges, atmospheres, psychic residue, and thought-forms. It renders the atmosphere of the place where it is done neutral, like an unpainted canvas. For this reason, it is used before a ritual taking place in an unconsecrated place. Do not be mistaken; the Banishing Ritual of the Pentagram does not turn an area into sacred space; it only purifies the area.

There is a surprisingly common misconception regarding this ritual in esoteric circles, some of which really should know better. These groups perform the Banishing Ritual of the Pentagram before *every* ceremony. When asked the reason, they say: "But the Hermetic Order of the Golden Dawn did it like this." Yes, they did—for a very good reason. Most of their ceremonies took place in hired halls; so they purified the room beforehand with the Banishing Pentagram Ritual. And that is the correct usage. I have known occult groups and practitioners who slavishly perform the pentagram rite before each ceremony, who then have asked me why their lodges or temples have no atmosphere, no resonance. This rite should never be performed in a consecrated temple of the Mysteries, unless it is being used after a ritual-working because the atmosphere needs cleansing. Otherwise, performing a banishing rite in a consecrated temple will remove that consecration and the accumulated energy lock, stock, and barrel.

What further confuses many sincere aspirants is when teachers advise the performance of the Pentagram Ritual as a daily exercise. Why would you banish every day? Or are you meant to perform it as a dummy run, without real energy, just to familiarize yourself with the ritual gestures? An example is where the adept W. E. Butler, in his excellent book *The Magician: His Training and Work*, recommends the daily practice of this rite, saying: "Here is Labour—but it is basic work, and without it the Work may not be done."[14] This proves that, in their writings, the sages are never as subtle as when they write simply.

In daily practice, what is being banished are the impurities in the practitioner's own temple—the body, inner vehicles, and aura—the sphere of sensation. Now, when I mention the subject of purity, most Western students go into neurotic mode. Here we need to be precise. Purity, from an esoteric viewpoint, is not about social mores or an individual's real or imagined sins. In occultism, purity has the same meaning it has in chemistry (and alchemy). It means something that is, itself, free from admixture with another substance, just as metal ore is smelted in fire to remove traces of all other compounds. A simple example of impurity occurs when, while preparing for a particular rite or meditation, your mind wanders onto domestic or social problems. This would technically be an impure intention.

In the performance of the Banishing Pentagram Ritual for subjective purification, it is your own interior state of consciousness that the invoked energies purify. All that you see, hear, touch, taste, and smell is formed of an elemental combination. In fact, the five senses themselves are expressions of the four elements and their quintessence in the human state. This purification is brought about by the pentagram—affirming by gesture and word the all-encompassing power of the Indivisible One and its abode in the human heart—and by the invocation of the archangels of the presence: Raphael, Michael, Gabriel, and Uriel. These four great princes of heaven are rulers of hosts of angels and are the regents of the elements themselves. ("Regents" is a technical term based upon the fact that these archangels rule on behalf of or represent the Divine to the elemental energies.) A sincere invocation of these archangels in the pentagram ritual brings your interior elemental states in line with those of creation, the spiritual world of Briah (which, be it remembered, is also the world of the archangels and where your higher self resides).

Some have asked: If various people in different locations are invoking the archangels at the same time, how can the archangels attend to them all? It is a valid question that shows you how deep is the hold of dualistic and form-habituated consciousness. Each angel is an aspect of the One Reality's *pleroma* (infinite fullness). All forces emanate from One Force; all beings are One Being! *Gabriel* means "God is mighty"; the name is from the same root as the name of the fifth sephira, Geburah. The Archangel Gabriel *is* the power of the One—not a being *with* the One's power, but a celestial expression of that power itself. As the One is omnipresent, so is Gabriel everywhere. In the world of creation, Gabriel is the power of God permeating all the worlds beneath Briah. When Gabriel is invoked in ceremony, God's power is present.

For the purposes of this ritual, you build thought-bodies by creative visualization for the archangels to use. This method of mental image-building used to be called "telesmatic imaging"; I only mention this so that, when you read older writings, you will know what is meant by the term. Essentially, you imagine anthropomorphic images— human features—and invest them with heavenly beauty and power. If these images are built up effectively and with sincerity, the archangels themselves will indwell the images and irradiate them, transfiguring them into eidolons of beauty, grace, and might beyond your present ability to imagine. It is most important that, after you have built the thought-forms of the regents of the elements, you visualize a thin beam of white brilliance descending from the Absolute into the head of the thought-image. This unites the form with the One Reality. This prevents it from becoming an empty shell that can be indwelt by one of the "impostors." It also unites the form with the source of all power so it is not dependent upon your thoughts and feelings for its continued existence. This very simple detail has far-reaching consequences. W.E. Butler when speaking of the thought-forms and images of the archangels, recommends the following:

> It will be remembered that we have formed four energy-charged thought-forms by the figures we have built [the pentagrams] at the four cardinal points of the compass. These forms we are now going to use as the focal points of the protecting barrier we have built, and we therefore build up behind them the telesmatic images of the four great Archangels. As the forces in the universe are in the last resort living forces, emanations of the Universal Mind, so we may think of these telesmatic images as the psychic means whereby we are able to make contact with the living and intelligent forces which are personified in the great Archangels. The *form* we build is a symbolic thought-form, but the *life* which fills it is the life of the great cosmic Being which we draw through that part of our nature which is in correspondence with him, or, to be more accurate, which is a part of him. As the old Initiates declared "There is no part of me which is not of the gods."[15]

THE BANISHING RITUAL OF THE PENTAGRAM

This ritual has never been accurately published in the public domain, until now.

1. Facing east, ascend the Tree of the Assiah and then invoke the Divine names of the Middle Pillar.

2. Make a firm intention that you are going to purify your personal sphere of sensation. Then perform the opening Qabalistic Cross (see page 17).

3. Say *Ateh, Malkuth, ve Geburah*, [pronounced Gevurah]; *ve Gedulah; le olham. Amen* [pro: Aum-ain]. (*Ateh*, meaning "Thou" is the pronoun in liturgical Hebrew for addressing deity alone. It is written by the first letter—*Aleph* (the Fool)—and the last letter—*Tau* (the World)—of the Hebrew alphabet. It is a way of saying: "Thou art the beginning and the end," or "Thou art alpha and omega,").

4. Perform the Banishing Earth Pentagram as described on page 167, visualizing that you draw the lines in blue-white light and that the star hangs in the air before you when completed. Then, with your hand, stab the center of the symbol, while simultaneously intoning the Divine name, *Yahveh*.

5. Turning to the right, trace a line in the same blue-white light to the right side, the south, of your aura. Repeat the pentagram and intone the Divine name, *Adonai*.

6. Turning to the right, trace a line in the same blue-white light to the west of your aura. Repeat the pentagram and intone the Divine name, *Eheieh*.

7. Turning again to the right, trace a line in the same blue-white light to the north of your aura. Repeat the pentagram and intone the Divine name, *Ateh Geburah le-olham Adonai.*

8. Turn right, tracing the radiant line so that you are facing east once more. The line has now joined up with the eastern pentagram and the circle is complete. Visualize the circle as extending above and below, until you stand within a sphere of glowing energy.

9. Build up the images of the four archangelic regents encompassing you (facing inward toward you) as you invite them into the sphere saying:

   Before me, Raphael—God heals; behind me, Gabriel (pronounced Gav-ree-ale)*—God is mighty; on my right hand, Michael—God is perfect* (pronounced Mi-ka-ale)*—; on my left hand, Auriel—God is light.*

10. Gesture to the relevant quarter (of your aura) as you mention each of the heavenly princes.

11. Continue, saying: *Around me flame the pentagrams; behind me shines the six-rayed star.*

12. Image the pentagrams shining about you, their radiance permeating you through and through, removing all defilements, without and within.

The six-rayed star is a reference to Tiphareth. It symbolizes the Macrocosm, as the star of five points represents the Microcosm. It also references the higher self. "Behind" means "above and beyond the incarnate personality."

To end the ritual, perform the closing Qabalistic Cross, sealing the transformative energies inside your aura. When the intention of the ritual is to purify a place, trace the pentagrams and circle around the entire space, so that the sphere encompasses it entirely. Image the archangels as having their stations at the circumference of the sphere at the cardinal points.

For two weeks, you should do the ritual physically. Then for two weeks, the ritual should be performed mentally, while you are still seated in meditation. When you have accomplished this, on the last day of your practice of this chapter's teachings, physically perform this ritual to purify your meditation area. This should be done only once, for reasons made clear above. Having completed the Banishing Rite of the Pentagram, perform the Rose-Cross ritual (see page 82) to fill the space with Tiphareth energy. Then, in your own words, dedicate the space to the Most Holy One. By this ceremony, prayer in action, your sacred space becomes a sanctuary, a holy place dedicated to the extension of the light.

12

HAIKAL CHOKMAH-NESTORAH: PART 2

Do therefore according to thy wisdom."

—1 KINGS 2:6

In chapter 8, you performed the first part of the Temple of Hidden Wisdom. Here, you will undertake the second part of the interior journey.

THE TEMPLE OF THE HIDDEN WISDOM, PART 2

Perform the Interwoven Light Exercises and invoke the Divine blessing, then build the gate between the worlds, the cedar doorway from which hangs the violet curtain, embroidered with the Tree of Life in silver. Focus on Da'ath while making your intention to journey to the Temple of the Hidden Wisdom. When the breeze arises, making the curtain billow, rise up from your physical body and step into the mists that lie beyond.

A warm breeze begins to disperse the mists that arose from the waters of the oasis during the cold desert night, as the Sun rises over the horizon of the east. For a few moments, you watch the Day Star as it ascends in beauty.

You hear the words: "Be thou welcome." You turn to the voice to see your companion, and joyfully greet him by name.

"The caravan awaits us," he reminds you. So together you go to prepare. You gather up your few belongings—sheep-fleece roll, cloak, sandals, and staff. Then saying "Good morning" to your *nephesh*, you untether the camel and mount up. With your companion, now mounted on his white camel, you rejoin the pilgrim caravan, escorted by its guardian knights. A shouted signal from the leader, and the caravan sets out across the desert again.

The morning passes uneventfully—golden sands, rolling dunes, and blazing Sun. At noon, the procession halts for a meal of fresh dates gathered from the oasis and a rest under cloaks spread for shade. Then, mounted again, you continue the journey.

The caravan has only journeyed for an hour or so when you hear a cry of alarm. Looking in the direction of the shout, you see a dark smudge on the southern horizon. All around you, people are dismounting and pulling their camels and horses into a circle. People are gabbling, the dromedaries are grunting with disquiet, and the horses are skittish. Still watching the south, where the smudge has grown in size, you realize it is traveling toward the party; you can see it is a great cloud of sand some fifty feet high and filling the horizon. Someone is tugging at your leg. You look down from your camel to see it's your companion trying to get your attention.

"Get down! he cries imperatively, "Sandstorm!"

Within moments you have obeyed and are pulling your dis-tressed camel into the circle of others. You notice that the sounds of your fellow pilgrims and their beasts are harder to hear, because, you realize, the whine of the approaching storm is increasing in volume. Like the others, you crouch down beside your seated camel, facing away from the "fury of the desert." Your companion motions, since he can't be heard over the storm, for you to pull your cloak up and over your head. The whine on the storm increases to a scream—and then it hits.

Heat, as the air is displaced, by tons of flying sand grains. Hot air, drying out your throat. Any part of your flesh that is exposed feels rasped as if by sandpaper. And pervading all the scream of the storm, a demonic wailing, as if all the djinn had escaped from Solomon's urn.

There is a shriek and, peering through the flying dust, you see that one of your party, a woman, is standing and screaming uncontrollably. Others try to pull her down, but she shakes them off with manic strength, then runs from the circle, disappearing into the raging storm.

Gradually, the sound decreases and the sandstorm begins to abate. When it has passed, everyone begins to emerge from the small mounds of sand that have covered them and their mounts. Everyone has sand-encrusted faces out of which squint red-rimmed eyes.

Quietly, the caravan reforms and mounts up. One of the guardian's steeds has gone, so two of the white-mantled knights have to ride double on one horse. The landscape has utterly changed, but the experienced caravan leader can still navigate by the Sun and stars. The caravan moves out, leaving the place of trial behind.

A little while later, it comes to an unexpected halt. Looking where your companion points, you see, half hidden by sand, the body of the woman who fled; half her face has been scoured down to the skull. The group pauses, each offering a silent prayer for the lost one, then quietly moves forward.

By late afternoon, a distant river is sighted, and the caravan increases its pace toward it. As you and the group draw closer, details become apparent. It is a wide river flowing across the plain. The land on the far side changes from desert to scrubland and—further in—to a fertile, green landscape. As you bear to the right, a stone bridge comes into sight. And on reaching it with the others, you lead your camel across. Remounting, the caravan continues through the scrubland, staying by the river as it meanders through the plain. There are occasional riverboats traveling on the broad river, their brightly colored sails catching the afternoon zephyrs; their crews and passengers wave as they pass.

In the distance, cliffs rear up out of the plain, with something gleaming, set just before them. Looking inquisitively at you companion, you point to it.

"Our destination," he replies with a bright smile. "The Temple of the Hidden Wisdom."

Everyone spurs their mounts on; the loping camels eat up the remaining distance. As the cliffs loom closer, a panorama of exquisite beauty is revealed. From the blue-gray cliff-tops cascades a mighty waterfall that creates scintillating rainbows. The waterfall is the source of the river's waters. And beside the fall, framed by the backdrop of the cliffs, rears a sacred edifice upon a grass-covered foothill. As the caravan approaches the base of the foothill, everyone's eyes gaze up at the holy temple.

Set back behind a low perimeter wall, the domed temple shines like a heavenly jewel fallen to Earth. Two great pillars rise before its portico—one white, the other black. The temple has glittering ornaments and details that are indistinct from this distance. Surmounting the rearing temple is a huge gold dome that blazes in the Sun's rays. It shines atop the sanctuary like a brilliant crown of fire.

Many people are encamped at the foot of the temple hill; already you can see over a hundred campfires around which people are preparing for the night. Other folk are still arriving—some like you, by desert caravan, others by boat, and a few who have journeyed in curtained litters with small retinues in attendance.

While your caravan makes its evening preparations, servants from the temple come and offer warm loaves and fresh vegetables. With the setting of the Sun, the stars come out. And lying in your bed, once more, you see arcing light-trails of shooting stars. And because you now know what they really are, you watch them with keen interest—although you are rather awed to see that the "fiery chariots" all converge upon the temple's dome, momentarily causing it to shine as if lit from within.

"Aye," says your companion from his bedroll, "All are coming, even the Great Ones. Now get you some sleep; tomorrow is high festival, the Convocation."

You roll up in your cloak, close your eyes . . . and dream a dream.

In the morning, the song of trumpets being sounded from the temple roof awakens you. You roll up your bed and, with the others, go to the river to make your ablutions. There is a sense of excitement in the air. Hurrying, you then turn to go up to the temple. But your Companion says,

"Your camel needs tending to."

At first you feel rebellious . . . but then you reflect on how your nephesh has borne you all this way, and relies on you. So you gather some vegetable scraps to add to the usual grain and, with fresh water, you give your mount a well-deserved breakfast. After giving it an affectionate pat, you go to rejoin the others who, you are surprised to see, are all in spotless white linen robes. And there is your companion too, also in a white robe, but over this he also wears a blue silk tunic. And there is a gold fillet on his head and a jeweled ring upon his index finger. You're rather startled; it is as if the sacred vestments have revealed more about your companion's true nature. Then he holds out a white linen robe for you and nods for you to put it on. You're about to ask a question, when he indicates, by placing a finger on his lips (the one wearing the ring), that the timing is inappropriate. Together with the others of your party, you prepare to ascend to the temple complex above.

The grass of the temple mound is soft underfoot and starred with small summer flowers. Reaching the top, you approach a low white wall whose gate is sheltered under a trellised archway covered by vines—deep purple grapes hang in clusters amid the green leaves. The gate is forever open to all true seekers.

Within, stretching all around the temple building, are gardens, smooth lawns, blossoming fruit trees, cool fountains. And at their ease within the gardens are women and men from every race upon the Earth—some alone, others in small groups engaged in deep conversation. And on every face there is an expression of gentle joy. Most are in white robes, like you, and a few are wearing blue silk tunics as well. Others are diademed with light.

"Behold, the spiritual Israel," says your companion.

"Are all these folk Jews then?" you ask.

"No," he replies, "There is a difference between the 'House of Israel' and the 'Children of Israel.' Membership in the one does not necessarily mean membership in the other. Only those who have passed beneath the vine-arch—who have distilled the wine of merit within their own souls—can truly be said to be of the Household."

"Who are those in blue and crowned with light?" you inquire.

Looking up to the temple, your companion answers, "Some are incarnate teachers, most are *maggidim*, inner teachers, while others yet are of the Incarnate Hierarchy—the seventy-two high priests—and beyond them, the *Lamed-Vav*, the thirty-six hidden sages who uphold the world."

"Then," you say excitedly, "You must be . . ."

"Yes," he replies drolly, "'Your *maggid*, your inner teacher." With this revelation, much now falls into place. He continues, "You now know my name and recognize the symbol of this ring, whereby to identify me. And this shall be our greeting . . . (here he gives a word or phrase which is known only to the two of you).

You are still pondering your companion's—no, your maggid's—comments when a great gong sounds from within the temple and reverberates from the high cliffs beyond. Three times it sounds; then three times more—then again—and finally, a lone, single note. The convocation begins!

Following your maggid, you approach the temple. It is raised up from the gardens by a wide platform, mounted by a flight of four steps. The twin great pillars that you saw from below rear up on either side of the entrance. That on the left is black obsidian, adorned with a spiraling garland of white lilies. On its cubical base is written: *Boaz*. The right-hand pillar is fashioned from whitest marble and garlanded with red roses; *Jachin* is carved upon its base. High above, on the cornerstone over the arched entrance, is incised the six-rayed star of love and unity, filled with gleaming gold. And beneath the star, in letters of fire, is written: "He that eats of the Tree of Life shall be like unto Us."

Passing beneath this arch, you find yourself in the *pronaos*, the vestibule. Its walls are of purple porphyry; there is a large brass bowl, some twelve feet across, filled with holy water. Following the example of your maggid, you immerse both your hands in the purifying water, then make a cup of them to bathe your face.

Two high silver doors stand open, leading from the pronaos; on either side of them, standing nearly twelve feet high, are two eagle-winged angels, each wielding a sword of celestial fire. As you come to this doorway, the angels gaze upon you with their deathless eyes. . . . Your maggid vouches for you and, seemingly satisfied, the heavenly guardians nod for you to pass within.

You enter into an immense blue chamber. Overhead is the great dome, deep blue and studded with golden stars. All around the walls, rising in tier upon tier, are rows of seats already nearly three-quarters full. You are so anxious following your maggid to your seats some halfway up that you don't take in the other details until you are seated. Once seated . . . you notice that the atmosphere pervading the temple is a strange combination of authentic sanctity mixed with the feeling of many dear friends who are delighted to be in one another's company again.

At the center of the white floor is a dark cloud! From it emanates great power, as if a thundercloud had been pulled down from the sky and affixed to the temple's floor. When all have taken their places, silence falls . . . and deepens as thousands of trained minds turn toward the Divine. Then, a single voice of unimaginable purity sings out:

> Holy art Thou, Lord of the Universe,
> Holy art Thou, Whom nature hath not formed,
> Holy art Thou, the Vast and the Mighty One,
> Lord of the Light and of the Darkness;
> May the blessing of the Prince of the Countenances
> descend upon us all.

You had not thought the temple dark at all, until the light descended. In response to the adoration of all present, a shaft of diamond fire lances down through the dome above and into the dark cloud in the midst. The light transmutes the dark cloud into a glory of white flames within which blazes a shining gold Tree with ten fruits of shimmering sapphire. Pure presence emanates from this glorious burning bush—celestial in nature, yet Divine in origin. Instinctively, you and all this gathered company—like so many before—put off your sandals and bow to that which the Tree betokens. . . .

As your vision draws closer, you can see the ornaments of the unconsumed Tree in more detail. Its branches are adorned with exquisite images of the ten archangels, the princes of the halls of heaven. Each of its seventy-two gold leaves is inscribed with a holy name. And within each of the sapphire jewel-fruits, you can see a sage wrapped in the bliss of Divine union.

"Know," comes the mind-speech of your maggid, "that the Tree of Life is a sacred standard, a means of attunement to the powers that, at the command of the One, brought the very cosmos into being."

Now, from the stars in the temple's dome, beams of light shine down upon the assembled. From the light beams fall variegated petals, a gentle rain of celestial *manna* to nourish the soul. The beams increase in size and intensity. They unite with the shaft that surrounds the Tree to become an all-encompassing incandescence. The Supernal Light engulfs all. The Supernal Light engulfs you. You dissolve into that light . . . and . . . you are with God.

After a time, when you have passed back into existence from eternity, you find yourself sitting once more in the *Haikal Chokmah-Nestorah*, in the company of your maggid and of all Qabalists, past and present, who serve the Most Holy One. Your hands are cupped around an object, a heavenly gift, to remind you that, henceforth, you are *known*. Treasure it.

In silence, the assembly departs from the temple proper, back into the vestibule, and so out into the gardens once more. It is evening. You walk alone for a little while, pondering upon what has been received from Above. Some time later, your maggid joins you. You stand together in companionable silence. Shooting stars arc across the sky from the temple behind you.

"Where are they going?" you ask your inner teacher.

"Why, home," he replies.

"Where do the Lords of Light live?"

The maggid gestures. For an instant, you see a vision of a sapphire mountain, so tall the clouds are its base. Upon the summit of the holy mountain is the golden City of Peace, and shooting stars are entering within it. The vision is gone.

"Within Jerusalem Above, the mother of us all; there they go in and out, before the Holy One, fulfilling what is the will by night and day." answers your maggid. "If it is willed, we may yet go there, when you're ready."

Finally, you suggest, "I had better return now; it's a long way back."

"Yes, as far as thought," he chuckles. "Come with me."

He leads you to a part of the temple gardens where, between two blossom trees, hangs a curtain. But *this* curtain is blue not violet, and the Tree of Life that adorns it is embroidered in *gold* threads.

"This gateway will always bring you directly back here, to the garden of the Temple of the Hidden Wisdom," your maggid tells you. "Back to the secret home of all Qabalists."

With tears of gratitude in your eyes, you reverence this inner teacher whom God has sent you; then you step through the blue curtain and back into the physical world of Assiah.

13

THE DWELLER IN ETERNITY

My God, the Neschamah which You have placed within me,
She is pure.

—JEWISH MORNING PRAYER

In *exoteric* religion, there is an ideological conflict between religions such as Judaism, Christianity, and Islam, which teach that God is a being, and those like Buddhism and Taoism that are "God-free," conceiving the Supreme Reality as a state. This conflict has led to much misunderstanding.

There are potential drawbacks to thinking of the Supreme Reality as either a person or a state. Because all images are concepts based on finite experience, they have certain subconscious associations we must undo through right reasoning. In conceiving the Absolute as a person, you embrace the implicit idea, in your subconscious, that some things may be given or withheld by that person—that some beings are favored and others not. On the other hand, when you conceive of the One Reality as a state, you imply that there is no personal relationship and that you must reach it unaided by the ineffable, solely by your own efforts.

This conflict is resolved by esoteric tradition. Some Christian mystics have taught that the three persons of the Trinity are finally absorbed into the Godhead. The Qabalah teaches that even divinity (Atziluth) is but a garment worn by the Absolute. In other words, any human-made image of the Absolute is bound to be finite. Those-who-know have assured us that the Absolute is both pure being (there is none other) and consequently, those who recognize it within themselves and unite with it enter into a state of being. And the Masters also declare that the Eternal is compassion itself. This is the unanimous record of all the sages.

How do these apparently high-flown metaphysics apply to us? At the most primordial level. In fact, at a level so deep that most people do not recognize its impact on all that we are. This level lies at the very root of the human condition itself.

Your relationship to the Absolute, to the Universal Self, is utterly subjective. If you subconsciously believe the Divine to be judgmental, vengeful, inflicting sickness and poverty; then it will be so for you. If you exchange outmoded forms of belief and come to know, as the ageless wisdom teaches, that the universe is, at heart, infinitely kind, that it wills all beings toward fulfillment, growth, and ultimate perfection, that it meets your every need, guides your every step on the way (if you let it), then so it will be with you. Moreover, as you believe God to be, so you will inexorably become, because you always make yourself in God's likeness. You may become vengeful, swift to anger, and judgmental; or you may become a guide, a healer, an encouraging smile along the way—or a thousand other possibilities. You may even "extend the Light."

The Macrocosm is reflected in the Microcosm. Some mirrors, like those at fun fairs, distort the image out of all resemblance to the reality they reflect. Other mirrors, by awareness and practice, polish and smooth their surfaces so that they become "an unspotted mirror of His power and the image of His goodness." But, in all cases, there is essentially only One Watcher gazing into each mirror and seeing there, through all human distortion, the Divine countenance veiled in time and space.

The Aura

The metaphorical mirror of which I wrote in the last paragraph, is our old friend, the sphere of sensation, the aura. In Western civilization, knowledge of the anatomy of the aura is one of the lost secrets. The aura appears as an ovoid of silvery light; it is because of its luminous and transparent appearance that texts on alchemy refer to the aura as the "glass vessel" of the art. It consists of concentric layers of varying density, with lines of force running through it. Much of your preliminary work has been focused upon the aura, using the indirect approach. (The purpose of the Interwoven Light Exercises is to purify and energetically stimulate your aura.) Now you will commence direct work on your aura.

Your aura should be visualized as extending an arm's length on either side of your material body and interpenetrating it; it will extend about three feet (thirty-six inches) above your head and below your feet. It is shaped like an egg, with the wider end over your head and the narrower under the feet.

Visualize the Tree of Life clearly within your aura, picturing it as you have practiced, with the spheres of the Pillar of Form on your right side and those of the Pillar of Force on your left. This is the opposite of the Tree as pictured macrocosmically, because the Macrocosm and Microcosm are mirror-reflections of one another and forever interacting. The centers—the sephiroth—should be seen as spheres, not as flat discs, approximately eight inches in diameter, so that the front of the sphere extends into the front of your aura and then back to its rear part. The spheres on the Middle Pillar enclose your spine. The sephiroth should be colored in the Queen scale of Briah. Because this particular color scale consists of the primary colors, it equates to those colors perceived by psychics and seers within the aura.

The physical body is the center of stability, the present moment, the ever-changing now. The front part of your aura extends before your body and belongs to the future of evolutionary time, while that which extends behind your body belongs to the evolutionary past. This has important ramifications on the path of initiation.

The twenty-two paths uniting the spheres are visualized in white light. They are strictly visualized as two-dimensional because they represent subjective experience, whereas the sephiroth are objective forces, being ten aspects of the One Reality. All subjective symbols are two-dimensional; to visualize them this way is an effective way of ensuring that they remain subjective. Whenever a symbol appears in perspective (in three dimensions), it may be assumed that objective elements are at work.

Having clearly established the Tree and its paths, you can now consciously link the Microcosm up with the Macrocosm. Funnel-shaped vortices of energy are projected from the centers on the Middle Pillar to the corresponding levels of the cosmos: that from Kether to the heights of heaven, that from Tiphareth to the Sun, that from Yesod to the Moon, and that from Malkuth to the heart of the Earth. Here, I do not refer to the physical bodies of the Sun, Moon, etc. I mean rather the levels of existence of which they are symbols.

In the ovoid of the aura, you can discern two distinct circuits of force. One is a downward-flowing current, energy coming in from the unmanifest through the Kether center and flowing down the Middle Pillar and through the Malkuth center, right down into the center of planet Earth.

The second circuit arises from Mother Earth and enters your aura through Malkuth. In evolved people, it passes through Kether and out into the unmanifest; in unevolved people, the rising current is absorbed by the various side spheres, until the triads become more developed. These two circuits pulsate, flowing and checking alternately. It is upon this energetic phenomenon in your aura that the Fountain Breath Exercise is built, utilizing an unconscious energetic function and developing and enhancing it. These two circuits express the human potential to become a conscious message of love from God to the Earth, and a prayer from the Earth back to God.

For the remainder of this book, readers practicing the exercises are encouraged not to perform any other esoteric ceremonies or engage in any magical workings other than those given here, because subtle, yet intense, pressure is now being brought to bear.

Initiation into the Mysteries of the secret wisdom is achieved by a twofold process similar to the building of the Channel Tunnel beneath the English Channel. When the Channel Tunnel was constructed, the work began at *both* ends, in England and in France. The two teams of workers bored through the sea bed from their own ends and eventually met in the middle, and . . . breakthrough!

It is the same with the initiatory process. The "channel" is begun at both ends—one from the earth-plane personality (your aspirations, exercises, and practices have a cumulative effect and build up a vortex of energy), the other on the inner planes (where your higher self, assisted by its various friends—masters, inner teachers, etc.—also builds a vortex of force). It is the successful meeting of these two that allows true initiation to occur. The function of an esoteric school is to try to produce the ideal conditions whereby these two vortices can meet and unite, resulting in . . . breakthrough!

When the two ends of the Channel Tunnel met beneath the sea, there was celebratory relief, because, no matter how good the mathematical calculations or the surveying engineers, there was always the possibility that they might be off. So too in initiation, there is this possibility. When the two ends do not fully engage, a *torte* occurs—a distorted channel requiring adjustment. Now this happens in most cases; human nature being what it is, few of us are perfect enough to be right on the mark. However, if the angle of the torte is too great, the initiatory influence will bypass the candidate.

So the purpose of this guideline is one of alchemical purity—as in purifying gold from any other trace elements—to ensure that no mixed energies fill your aura. You are therefore asked, for the time being, to refrain from solo or group magical work. This does not apply to personal religious devotions or observances. But if you belong to a group that combines worship with magical work (spiritualist, shamanic, Druidic, Wiccan, etc.), for the time being you must be clear that, while you can engage in the worship element at this stage, you must withdraw from the magical workings.[16] This advice is not a judgment on any other practices; it is simply that, for this critical stage of your Qabalistic work, the influence of your higher self must be the only thing to permeate and saturate your being. This is accomplished by the cumulative effect of your current work, traditionally known as the "wine of merit," and expressed by the esoteric ceremony that follows.

Invocation of the Holy Guardian Angel

The intention of this ceremony is to invoke illumination from your higher self, from your spiritual consciousness. The higher self is sometimes called the Holy Guardian Angel or the Golden Dweller in Eternity. It is the *ruach* in Tiphareth, the real "I" behind your previous incarnations. It is the superconscious link between the Divine and mundane levels of awareness. It is the abiding self, of which the incarnate personality is but a fraction. It is the immortal spirit as distinct from the incarnate soul.

In the past, your higher self has guided you upon the path of evolution, but you have been unaware of its presence, except, perhaps, in times of crisis or exaltation. Previously, its guidance has manifested through intuitive promptings and auspicious coincidences. Now, you may consciously reach out to your higher self and invite its redemptive and trans-- forming influence into your life. Astrologically, the higher self is represented by your natal Sun sign; your personality is represented by your individual Moon sign.

The following ceremony ritually expresses the desire to "Know thy-self" (*Gnothi seauton*), written over the portals of the Mystery temples in ancient Greece. Although the serious working of this ceremony is uplift-ing and inspiring, it will also, in time, bring to light those areas of your personality that need work. And the way to work on those areas, as pre-viously taught, is to identify which sephira on the Tree is the required medicine. Meditate on that sephira, and so bring its influence to bear upon your personality.

Remember, however, that for an effective result when working with one of the sephiroth on the black or white pillar, you must also meditate upon its polar opposite and then harmonize and integrate their energies within you. To perform the completion stage, meditate upon the sephira on the Middle Pillar that completes the functional triad of the other two—e.g., Chesed, Geburah, then Tiphareth. In this way, you bring a bal-anced personality to the Great Work as an offering to God.

Each of the sephiroth has a magical image, a pictorial representation that, through meditation, comes to be identified by your subconscious with the sephira concerned. These images are mundane expressions of the shining Divine archetypes by which the physical world has been projected into materialization. Tiphareth alone, because of its crucial importance on the Tree, has three magical images: a child, a sacrificed god, and a priest-king.

Because of the deep-rooted tendency of the Yesodic ego to identify the higher with itself rather than the other way around, the magical image of the child is far better suited for use at this stage. It also indicates that the process of enlightenment is a gradual one. The ecstatic heights of the Mountain of Illumination are not for beginners or even apprentices. We all need to learn how to walk before we can run, and how to run before we can fly! To build an affinity with the magical image of the child, you will find it fruitful to contemplate pictures of the Divine child archetype. Images of the child in the stable at Bethlehem, the baby Krishna, or the infant Horus of Egypt are most useful when you remember that these images are poetic representations of your own spiritual reality. The *Zohar* tells how the Archangel Metatron (Enoch, the first self-realized human being) instructed the sages while wearing the form of a child; this is one of the reasons why Metatron is titled the Youth in the heavenly court. The young Jesus of Nazareth did the same to rabbis in the temple.

The Divine name used in the following ritual is that by which the Divine is adored in Tiphareth: *Yahveh-Eloah-ve-Da'ath.* The Divine names define and describe the aspect of the infinite One, which is expressed through the sephira to which it is assigned. As such, the holy names are the true passwords to the real initiatory grades within the ten sephiroth. They are the true words of power, because they express the omnipotent activities of the One Power. You can learn much by spelling out the letters of a Divine name with the tarot keys and then meditating on the resulting tableau. The essential meaning of the name you will invoke here, *Yahveh-Eloah-ve-Da'ath,* is at one with the meaning of the Hindu phrase, *Sat-Chit-Ananda,* which means "existence, knowledge, bliss."

In the working that follows, the various skills you have been practicing are brought together. These "notes" will now make one song. "My songs will I make of Thy Name, Oh Thou Most Highest . . ." [17]

THE RITE OF THE HOLY GUARDIAN ANGEL

Ideally, this ceremony should be performed on a Sunday, the day of Tiphareth, the Sun. Cover your altar with a gold or orange cloth. Behind the burning lamp of the presence, place upright the tarot Key XIV, Temperance. Upon each side of the lamp, place three gold or orange candles—six in all, the number of Tiphareth. Burn frankincense or amber incense.

Make a purification ablution and then put on your robe. Enter your sacred space and kindle the lamp with the usual invocation (*"From Thee, O Effulgent One . . .* , see page 152), then, using a taper, light the six candles and the incense from the lamp's flame.

Enter a meditative state: perform the relaxation exercise on page 15 and establish the 4:2:4 breathing cycle (see page 16). Ascend the Tree of the body, then do the Interwoven Light Exercises (see page 87). Then focus exclusively on Tiphareth and image its golden radiance raying out through your body and filling your aura, so that you are a being fashioned of, and encompassed by, vibrant golden light. Perform the opening Qabalistic Cross (see page 17) to seal this light in your aura. This sets the tone of the ritual.

1. Going to the east, trace in gold light the invoking pentagram of earth. From the top angle at your head, trace down and across until your hand is level with your left hip; then trace the other lines until your hand is back at the top (this is the opposite of the Banishing Pentagram of Earth); then point into the center of the gold star and declare: *In the Divine Name of Yahveh-Eloah-ve-Da'ath, and by the Sign of the Pentagram, I open the Portal of the East.*

2. See the eastern gate opening, then trace a line from the center of the star to the south and repeat the pentagram there. Repeat this in the west and north, finally returning to the east, where the line of energy goes into the center of the first star—(the serpent swallows its tail) and the magic circle is complete.

3. Visualize the four archangels of the presence standing before each portal and facing in toward the circle wherein you stand. Use anthropomorphic images, human forms with mighty eagles' wings. Image them approximately twelve feet in height, their outstretched wings crossing one another, so that the circle is encompassed by these great heavenly powers.

4. Image Raphael in the east as golden-winged, robed in blue, and bearing the scepter-wand, the rod of power.

5. Image Michael in the south, winged with peacock feathers, clad in armor, and wielding the flaming sword.

6. Image Gabriel in the west, violet-winged, robed in silver, and holding the chalice of form.

7. In the north, image Auriel, dark-robed, rainbow winged, and holding the golden pentacle that is platter and shield.

8. Build up these images until they acquire a peculiar sense of independence; then, in your own words, welcome these celestial princes. Always invoke "to the eyes" of the image. These ensouled images of the archangels perform the same functions as would a team of officers in an esoteric lodge. By establishing contact with the elemental regents (as these archangels are also called), you simultaneously link up with those aspects of yourself that they personify.

Having linked with the great deep within you (your subconscious), you now aspire to the Eternal (the superconscious). You do this by calling upon the name and power of the "angel of the operation," in this case, Great Michael, Captain of the Heavenly hosts, archangel of the sphere of *Shemesh,* the Sun. Build his image over the altar, using that of tarot Key XIV, Temperance. The archangel is robed in white, with the seven-pointed star of the Great Work on his breast and haloed with the Sun. His great scarlet-and-blue wings overshadow you. High up above him gleams the thousand-rayed diamond crown of Kether. The archangel holds the flaming torch of *Aud* in one hand, and the vase of the art in the other. Build up this image that will be the channel for his power and then vibrate (chant) his name: *MI-KA-ALE.* When the presence of the archangel is felt, pause and gather your strength for the working itself. Now you approach the *pegasus*, the climax, of the ceremony.

9. Strongly visualize the image of the Child of Light while you intone the Divine name in Tiphareth: *Yahveh-Eloah-ve-Da'ath.* Then affirm your intention: to receive illumination from your higher self.

10. Holding your mind fixed upon the image of the child, remain mentally poised, like a hawk hovering in one place despite the winds. As the hawk, although appearing motionless, requires strength and effort to ride the wind while holding its position, so your consciousness, wrapped in the ecstasy of true invocation, must hold its poise, its intention.

11. Upon the four-squared foundation of your quartered magic circle, you have built a pyramid by your thought and effort. Now, standing upon its summit, at the secret fifth gate, reach up to the source of all, to the Absolute that is the Supreme Rapture. Wait, poised, aflame with aspiration. Then say: *I think like a god, I speak like a god, I act like a god; for I am Thy Child, Oh Thou Who art the Living God. Thou art in me and I am in Thee, forever.*

You may reach this apex in the ceremony many times without any apparent results, but each time you work it, your subconscious mind is influenced by it. Each time you repeat it, the ritual builds a power within you. And a day will come when, as you aspire toward the Child of Light, irradiated by the beams of Kether, the burning energy of the secret force will surge through you, the visualized scene will vanish, and you will find yourself standing in the sphere of the Sun. You will be encompassed by the glory of that Sun, as, for a moment outside of time, you become mystically identified with the Eternal Child, and upon each side will unfurl the healing wings of glory. In that moment of the holy Now, your consciousness will be transfigured, as you become spiritually aware—a child of the Most High—as you become consciously immortal. It is written, "They that wait upon the Lord shall renew their strength, they shall mount up with wings, as eagles."[18]

Of course, this new mode of consciousness is but a foretaste. At first, it is momentary and sporadic. But with practice and increasing skill, it will stabilize until you come to know why it has been said, "This is My beloved Child, this day have I begotten thee." On that day, you will become more than *Homo sapiens*; you will become *Homo spiritualis*. The ultimate goal of the Mysteries is divinization.

Having received all that you can at this time, you now begin to refocus on the physical plane. In all invocatory magic, you ascend in stages to keep consciousness steady, and you descend in the same way. The symbols used to go up are also used to come down, but in the reverse order. This is what is meant by the Mystery phrase: "If you go out by the Pylon Gate, you must return by it."

12. Intoning the Divine name with awareness of whose name is being uttered, build the image of the Divine child, thus adoring the Absolute through that symbol.

13. Recall the image of the angel of the operation, Michael of the Sun, and thank him for his assistance.

14. Invoke the blessing of the Absolute upon all who have assisted you. At each portal you salute, thank the archangel of the quarter; draw the Banishing Pentagram of Earth, and say: *In the Divine name of Yahveh-Eloah-ve-Da'ath, and by the sign of the pentagram, I close the portals of the east/south/west and north.*

15. Repeat this at each of the portals of the magic circle.

16. Under the authority of the Divine name of the rite, bid all spirits to return to their own proper realms.

17. Descend the Assiatic Tree of the body, centering your consciousness firmly in each sphere. Reciting The Pattern of the Trestleboard (see page 120) is very helpful, particularly if you *have* touched superconscious levels.

18. Perform the closing Qabalistic Cross to seal your aura and return all images back into subconscious latency.

19. Stamp your foot on the ground to signify that your full awareness is once again within the physical realm.

20. Extinguish the six candles, allowing the sacred flame to burn a little longer while disrobing.

Immediately write up any subjective reactions you may have to the impact of working this ceremony in your journal.

MIRRORING THE MACROCOSM EXERCISE

Begin with the relaxation exercise on page 15, followed by the opening Qabalistic Cross. Perform the Banishing Ritual of the Pentagram (see page 172) and the Interwoven Light Exercises (see page 87). Build the Middle Pillar (see page 49) and perform the Fountain Breath Exercise (see page 99).

1. Starting from Malkuth, ascend the Tree of the material body, building the sephiroth in the Queen scale of Briah.

2. Refocusing on Malkuth, send a spiraling vortex of indigo-colored energy from your personal Malkuth center downward

into the very heart of the planet. Image the vortex as a cone of spiraling energy. The point of the cone is, in all cases, within your center. As the cone spirals, it extends in circumference until it reaches the planetary center and unites with it.

3. From your Yesod center, send a spiraling vortex of silver energy outward into the astral level, imaged as a full Moon in a violet sky.

4. From your Tiphareth center, send a spiraling vortex of gold energy outward into the mental level, imaged as a blazing noonday Sun in an orange sky.

5. From your Crown center, from Kether, send upward a spiraling vortex of pure white energy, like an inverted cone, into the height of heaven.

6. Abide in the resultant state of awareness.

7. Perform at least ten more cycles of the Fountain Breath Exercise, noting the difference.

8. Descend the Tree of Assiah.

Perform the closing Qabalistic Cross and write up the experience in your journal. Once a week, work this ceremony as described and note your subjective reactions in your journal.

14

THE IMMANENCE

The heart is the hub of all sacred places;
go there and roam at will.

—CARROLL DUNHAM AND IAN A. BAKER,
TIBET: REFLECTIONS FROM THE WHEEL OF LIFE

In recognition of this sentiment in the above quote, I now impart to you a precious spiritual treasure. It is a profound interior practice by which adepts attain their illumination and by which the highest magics are performed. The teaching is called the Temple of the Heart, or sometimes the Interior Sanctuary. It leads to the realization of the essential unity of the Macrocosm with the Microcosm, for Qabalah, you will remember, is often called the Way of Unification. Unlike pathworkings and inner journeys that lead to *different* realms of being, the locus of The Temple of the Heart is you. The varying levels of the meditation represent your own totality as a sacred human.

W. E. Butler wrote the following in his book *The Magician, His Training and Work*. Although Butler here refers to an adept mage, the teaching is still applicable to us all, in varying degrees.

For the adept-magician, though he may use the age-old ceremonies, does not *depend* on them. The observances which were the outward, visible symbols of inner states of emotion, mind and spirit, have, through the training he has undergone, been withdrawn into and made components of his inner consciousness. Then the Preparation of the Place is effected within the Ring-Pass-Not, the limiting boundary of his own aura, the Angel of the Operation is invoked therein, and the mystical temple is built in his mental sphere. Then into this "temple not made with hands," there descends the Divine *Shekinah*, the Glory of the Eternal, and She abides over the seat of Justice between the Cherubim in the Holy of Holies of the magician's heart.[19]

THE TEMPLE OF THE HEART, PART 1

This interior practice is divided into sections, each of which should be practiced until the imagery becomes established in your mind— until it becomes automatic within your subconscious. The reason for this is that each section is dependent for its effectiveness to transform on the sections that precede it. Once a section has been established, you can pass through it with proficient speed.

Before you begin, seal your aura with the opening Qabalistic Cross (see page 17) and perform the relaxation exercise on page 15. Establish the 4:2:4 breathing cycle (see page 16), then, ascend the microcosmic world of Assiah, the Tree of your body (see page

84). Having so risen in consciousness, perform the Interwoven Light Exercises (see page 87) in their plenitude, then use the Fountain Breath Exercise (see page 99) to immerse and saturate your physical and subtle vehicles in the alchemical fountain of white brilliance.

1. On an inhalation, when the radiant energy arises within the Middle Pillar, from Malkuth toward Kether, restrain the ascending force within Tiphareth. Think of this as causing a point of ruby-colored light to appear, like a small jewel, within the golden sphere of Tiphareth.

2. Refocus your consciousness in Kether and, on an exhalation, direct the white brilliance from Kether onto the ruby point in Tiphareth. From the impact of this descending light, the ruby point expands with a spiral motion, like the unfolding petals of a flower, to become an open ruby rose, glowing at the heart of golden sphere of the Sun.

3. Raise your awareness into Kether again (rising from Tiphareth through Da'ath, and back to the crown chakra) into the all-pervasive brilliance of exalted consciousness. Image the following visualization:

Within the white light, you approach a pylon gate. It is fashioned of yellow marble and covered with hieroglyphs that are a record of your long journey. One day, this chronicle of your Spirit will be read by you. Upon the lintel of the gate is the winged Sun-disc of Egypt—the disc of thrice-refined gold. The outstretched wings are scarlet feathers with royal-blue highlights. Through the open gateway lies a scene bathed in the light of the noonday Sun. The gate stands at one end of an avenue, flanked on either side by ram-headed sphinxes, that leads through an open gate into a high-walled garden.

Walk the avenue and enter the garden. It is always summer here. The flowers are in bloom, releasing their heady perfume and scenting the garden; insects and birds may at times be present. There are two oblong pools, one on either side, separated by a small causeway—a shallow ramp that leads up to the next level. The pool on your right is filled with cool, silvery, lunar waters; the pool to your left contains warm, golden, solar waters. Both pools are adorned with water flora. You can also see that the pools are fed by separate cascades that emerge from the terrace above. Before going any further, it is wise to partake of the waters of the Moon and those of the Sun.

The causeway leads up to a terrace upon which rears the edifice of the Temple of the Heart. How you perceive the temple is individual. It may resemble a physical building you know; it may be a composite—a mixture of architectural styles; or it may be very unusual. However it appears under the veil of form, it will be scarlet-crimson in color (a ruby-red like a red presence-lamp lit from within) and there will also be a rose window above its entrance. This entrance is *always* open.

Return through the walled garden . . . along the ram-sphinx avenue . . . and back through the pylon gate into the white brilliance of Kether. The ruby rose swirls and closes, becoming a small point of ruby light in the golden sphere of your Tiphareth center, then vanishes.

Perform the Fountain Breath Exercise to distribute the energies throughout your entire organism. *This is very important.*

Finally, descend the Tree of Assiah while reciting the The Pattern on the Trestle Board (see page 120), synchronizing the appropriate declaration to its sephira as your focus of consciousness descends the Tree to Malkuth.

THE TEMPLE OF THE HEART, PART 2

Begin as before, with the Qabalistic Cross, the relaxation exercise, and the 4:2:4 breath cycle. Ascend the subjective Tree in Assiah, perform the Interwoven Light Exercises and image the point of red light unfolding into the ruby rose. Now, focused in Kether, pass through the gateway, along the avenue, and into the walled garden. (Consider that the word "paradise" is from the Persian, meaning "a garden.") Having partaken of both the lunar and solar pools, walk up the ramp between them onto the terrace and look up at The Temple of the Heart. When it feels appropriate, enter.

The temple is oblong and oriented from west—the entrance where you now stand—to east. The floor is fashioned of alternating squares of red and gold. The walls are the same color as the temple when seen from without, like a presence lamp lit from within. The high roof is supported by eight gold pillars standing in two rows, four on either side. The eastern end of the temple appears as a gold wall. Against this wall there rises a jeweled throne on a dais flanked by two low offering altars. The altar to your right is white with red roses upon it; the other, on your left, is black and bears pure white lilies.

The next stage requires practice. Upon the throne, build a thought-form of an ideal being that, for you at this stage, represents the All-Good. You may choose a God-form from one of the ancient pantheons of deities, or a spiritual master whose life speaks to you of the Divine's wisdom, power, and love. Build the form by thought, until it becomes as defined and translucent as a crystal. You are building a *mask of God*, a form through which you can relate to the Absolute in an intimate way. Practice (you may take as many sessions as you need), until the jeweled throne is occupied by a transparent image of the ideal being some twelve feet in height with *closed* eyes.

When completed, in your own words, give praise to the light in the person of the named ideal being. In response, see a narrow beam of white brilliance, as intense and potent as a laser, descending from the infinite height into the vacant thought-form. The beam enters the head of the thought-form, fills it and irradiates it, like the Sun suddenly emerging from behind a cloud. The thought-form now appears in strong, shimmering colors appropriate to its nature. The eyes open . . . incense drifts through the temple . . . and the Divine now beholds you through one of its aspects. Spend some time reflecting upon, and communing with, this epiphany of the One.

Once this stage has been completed, the thought-form of the ideal being is contacted, becoming a living eidolon—what was called, in Egypt "a living double of the God." Always ensure that you see the beam of white light connected to the ideal being. And from now on, whenever you enter or leave, reverence the enthroned ideal being, thus: *Hail [name], Deity of the Temple of my Heart!*

Withdraw and perform the closing practices as in Part 1.

THE TEMPLE OF THE HEART, PART 3

Commence as before. Then, from your subjective Kether center, pass through the gate, down the avenue, and into the garden. Take refreshment from the pools of Moon and Sun. Enter the Temple of the Heart and, on reaching the east, reverence the now-living eidolon of the ideal being. Then image the following visualization:

Having saluted and addressed the enthroned deity, turn to your left and walk past the black altar with the white lilies toward the nearest pillar of the left-hand row. You discover that the eastern wall is, in fact, a gold screen. Turn right behind the screen and see that, set into the real east wall, there is a small alcove that lies in direct alignment to the ideal being upon the other side of the screen. The alcove is a rounded arch, inside which three gold steps lead up to a dark veil or curtain. There is a symbol above the arch. Once you stand atop the third step with the veil before you, know this: behind you all are mind-created appearances, your own inner world and conditions, the outer world peopled with individuals, locations, and circumstances. Time, history, and linear perception are fleeting bubbles thrown up by the mind-stream of consciousness. They are ephemeral, fleeting, and transient. But, beyond this veil, in the sanctuary of the Temple of the Heart, lies that which alone endures. Resolve to return to the source that is also the ultimate goal to which all life is moving and speak the words: *Adonai-Interna*. Then part the veil that separates the many images from the One Light.

At first, within, there is thick darkness, like a dark cave, but you persist and see, at the center, a still gold flame in a halo of rainbow light. The halo is an expression of the unconditional love of the higher self and of the supreme self that is forever one with the Eternal. The immanence (for such it is) may appear as an unflickering candle flame—and indeed, should all the storms of the world beat upon it, they could not cause it to move. And therefore, this place is also known as the Central Stillness. This is the immanence, the abiding indwelling of the Divine. It is given many names by those who have sought to share it with other seekers: the Inner Light, the Christ within, the Buddha nature. It is the flame shining from the lamp held by the Hermit in tarot Key IX; for the Hermit is the pictorial symbol of the Supreme Self, which is indivisible, yet unique. Now, alone with the All-One, who is your deepest identity and the All-Good, speak the words: *Lord, Thou art I Am.*

All that you will ever need will issue from this light. All healing emanates from this light. All abundance pours through this light. All knowledge is imparted by this light as the Voice of Silence. Listen; to hear it, assume the mental attitude of "Speak, Lord, your servant hears." This light is the one portal to the supreme self and to *samadhi*, the unutterable bliss of union with the Divine.

The Lord is in His holy temple—let all the worlds fall silent before Him.

After your session, withdraw from the timeless back into the relative by passing out of the sanctuary through the veil. Now that you know the way, it can never be denied you. Descend the three gold steps of the alcove, turn left and walk to the end of the screen. Pass around it into the temple. Walk by the white altar with the offering of red roses on it, and stand again before the ideal being, the mask of God. Give reverence, for all is sacred unto the

One. Pass from the temple into the garden and walk under the noonday Sun, between the ram-headed sphinxes, to the pylon gate of the crown.

Close down as before and go into the outer world to live your life in the light of what you received in the temple of *your* heart.

He is One and One Alone,

rest under the shadow of His wings;

and may Light by extended upon you . . . and through you.

EPILOGUE

This visualization will form a fitting end to the pathworkings of this book. Before you begin, seal your aura with the opening Qabalistic Cross formula (see page 17) and perform the relaxation exercise on page 15. Establish the 4:2:4 breathing cycle (see page 16), then ascend the microcosmic world of Assiah, the Tree of your body (see page 84).

THE PAVILION

You rise in meditation from pure, formless awareness into a natural scene in late spring. You are in a meadow, upon a gentle hill, beside the edge of a forest. The warmth of the Sun pervades you; an abundance of plant life, in leaf and blossom, surrounds you. It is good. Then, you look down upon a small village nestled at the bottom of the hill. You watch the village folk engaged in the cycle of their daily lives, coming and going, absorbed in their own matters.

After a little while, you turn about and enter the forest. You mark the contrast of light, passing from the bright radiance of the meadow into the emerald-suffused illumination of the forest. The trees rear up like pillars, springy moss carpets underfoot; it is as if you had entered some vast cathedral of nature. The leaf mold crushed by your walking feet releases a fragrance like an incense of the earth, and all around you the birdsong resounds like an invisible choir. Walking in this natural yet holy place, you feel soothed, refreshed.

As you progress, you occasionally see a forest creature—perhaps a stag or rabbit, a cuckoo or a jay. And out of the corner of your eye, you can momentarily glimpse the subtle denizens of this forest: gnome or elf, nature spirit or dryad. Through the birdsong, a new sound emerges, a sweet rippling sound. You come to a swift-flowing stream whose pure waters meander through the forest. You follow the waters upstream as they wind their way through the trees. Ahead, the light is getting brighter. You realize there is an opening in the tree canopy ahead.

You emerge into a glade set amid the forest. The first thing you see is a black tent. It is set upon a grassy hummock covered with a profusion of flowers. From its side well up the waters that feed the stream. The tent's guy ropes are vermilion and staked into the ground with gold tent pegs in the form of the Hebrew letter *Vav*. The central tent pole is surmounted by a golden trident shape, the holy letter *Shin*. You remember this tent from the oasis. Great power, arising out of deep serenity, surrounds the tent like a wall of rainbow light and you can sense invisible presences all around, as if unseen guards kept watch.

Yet, despite the warding, you feel drawn, compelled, to walk up the small rise to the tent. Close up, the cloths of the tent are not black at all. They are formed out of a curious living darkness, something for which there is no adequate description. You walk around the tent, coming to the entrance flap—a blue curtain embroidered the letters of the Shem, the four-lettered title of the One Reality. What, you wonder, could lie beyond an entrance guarded by the name of God? You consider retracing your steps away from this place. But something within you, and yet also beyond you, calls you forward. You draw the blue curtain aside . . . . And pass within.

The tent is larger on the inside than it is on the outside, but of comfortable, intimate dimensions. Its carpets are of Eastern richness, woven in the colors of existence: red and blue and purple and gold. The sides are hung with rich tapestries depicting, in jewel-like tones, motifs of spiritual attainment and symbols of transformation. You could spend years just studying these woven picture books. A veil of unadorned white linen, a stark simplicity in the midst of this richness, curtains off the far end of this pavilion (opposite the entrance). And before the snowy veil shines a hanging lamp, the tent's only illumination, in which burns the secret fire.

You feel the need to rest a while, to acclimatize to the rarified atmosphere of this curtained pavilion. For it feels as if your inner senses are being purified and expanded by some unseen influence. It is as if your vibration rate is being increased and enhanced—but oh so delicately. Feeling more adjusted now, you try to identify the source of this benign influence. You conclude that, although it seems to come from all around you, as if the whole tent were bathed in it, its principal focus seems to flow from the area hidden by the linen veil. Then, as if your own inner recognition were a spoken signal, the area behind the veil slowly brightens

As concealment after concealment is withdrawn . . . the brightness increases, by degree, till it shines as a high white effulgence, like moonlight upon snow-crowned mountains. A gentle wind springs up inside the tent; it carries the perfume of frankincense, as if the orchard of paradise were on fire. The veil billows back . . . and before the naked glory, you drown in its light.

Yet, although the shining causes the eyes of your soul to close, it simultaneously causes the eyes of your spirit to open. And with that opening, there is likewise an opening of your spiritual hearing. So that sight and sound weave together, thrilling with the reception of one epiphany, which bestows one understanding. And you see and know no mortal Sun, but one that shines for everlasting, the Heart of All Brightness.

You know this to be the holy Shekinah—the Divine presence. For some, it appears as the Ark of the Covenant, for others as the Grail; perhaps there are as many masks for it as there are beings. But for now, it is the cup with which Melchisadech initiated Abraham into the Qabalah.

This patriarch had been, until then, named Abram; but with his initiation, he received a new name. The letter *Heh* ("a window") was seeded into his old name to indicate that, henceforth, he was transparent to the light. The cup brought by Melchisadech holds the supernal dew that is the life of worlds. This chalice symbolizes the ultimate covenant, the unbreakable promise that all beings shall ultimately return to the Absolute, for it is present within everybody and everything. In many, it is veiled, but only for a while. A time will come to each one when it will be known in all its splendor and bliss as clear, radiant divinity. It is said that the children of Abraham shall number as the grains of sand, but that the Children of Melchisadech shall number as the stars of heaven.

Does the priest-king of the Most High come now? Does, he bring the cup for you to drink? If not now, then assuredly at some other time he will come. For, in truth, you always partake of it, although mediated by others, with every breath you take. It is only a matter of when you are able to drink of it consciously, directly, and nakedly. With the awareness of what *your* life's sustenance is comes the awareness of your real identity. And herein lies the sublime Mystery, for it is the No-thing of which nothing can be said.

As the snowy veil falls back to conceal the *Kavod,* the glory, a new, yet ancient, knowledge awakens in your mind. This knowledge clothes itself in words as you leave the tent and walk beside a silent swan that swims downstream, back through the forest, and to the meadow where you began.

You know now the name of the pavilion, the small back tent. It is the Tabernacle of Peace. You know it is the secret abode of the Shekinah—not secret because others aren't told of it, but because few can perceive it. Only those with purity and right motivation can find it.

You know now that, sometimes, the Tabernacle of Peace comes to rest upon a city. It may be Jerusalem, Lhasa, Rome, or New York. Sometimes the Tabernacle of Peace comes to rest upon a hermit's cave, or a garden, or a deathbed, or a room in North London, or a group for one meeting. You now know that when you have made real, not fantasized, progress on the path, when you close your eyes in meditation or prayer, the Tabernacle of Peace may spontaneously form about you. For the Shekinah only comes to those who seek to walk with God.

Long ago, when the world was young, a prophecy was made. It foretold a time when the tent of the Shekinah—her Tabernacle of Peace—would cover all the Earth . . .

May this prophecy swiftly come to pass, and in your lifetime. Amen.

NOTES

1 Christine Hartley, *The Western Mystery Tradition*, (Welligborough, UK: Aquarian Press, 1986), p. 150.

2 Dion Fortune, *Moon Magic* (York Beach, ME: Samuel Weiser Inc., 1999), p. 155.

3 Garth Fowden, *The Egyptian Hermes* (Princeton, NJ: Princeton University Press, 1986).

4 Dion Fortune, *Mystical Qabalah* (London: Ernest Benn Ltd., 1935), p. 17.

5 Jacob Boehme, *The Signature of All Things* (n.p.: Thomas Clarke, 1969), p. 23.

6 Alipili, "The Salt of Nature Regenerated," in *Hidden Symbolism of Alchemy and the Occult Arts* by Herbert Silberer (New York: Dover, 1971).

7 Albert Pike, *Morals and Dogma of the Ancient and Accepted Scottish Rite of Freemasonry* (Richmond, VA: L. H. Jenkins, Inc., 1950), p. 287.

8 Lapidus, *The Secret Book of Artephius*, 12th-century translation in the British Library.

9 Israel Regardie, *The Art of True Healing* (Novato, CA: New World Library, 1991), p. 6.

10 Anna Kingsford, *The Perfect Way*, Lecture 9, (n.p.: Sun Publishing Co., 1996).

11 Paul Foster Case, *True & Invisible Rosicrucian Order* (York Beach, ME: Weiser Books, 1985).

12 John 1:9, 14.

13 Dion Fortune, *Psychic Self-Defense* (London: The Antiquarian Press, 1971), pp. 184–185.

14 W. E. Butler, *The Magician: His Training and Work* (n.p.: Melvin Powers Wilshire Book Co., 1969), p. 169.

15 Butler, *The Magician: His Training and Work*.

16 If any crisis or emergency occurs, then use the methods given in *The Sacred Magic of the Angels* (Weiser Books, 1996), as these invoke celestial influences alone.

17 Psalms 9:2.

18 Isaiah 40:31.

19 Butler, *The Magician: His Training and Work*, p. 152.

RECOMMENDED READINGS AND CDS

Books

Butler, W. E. *Lords of Light*. Rochester, VT: Destiny Books, 1990.

———. *Magic & the Qabalah*. Northampton, UK: The Aquarian Press, 1978.

Case, Paul Foster. *The Tarot*. Los Angeles, CA: Builders of the Adytum, 1990.

———. *True & Invisible Rosicrucian Order*. York Beach, ME: Weiser Books, 1985.

Fortune, Dion. *Moon Magic*. York Beach, ME: Weiser Books, 1999.

———. *Secrets of Dr. Taverner*. Marble Hill, GA.: Ariel Press, 1989.

Goddard, David. *The Sacred Magic of the Angels*. York Beach, ME: Weiser Books, 1996.

———. *Tower of Alchemy*. York Beach, ME: Weiser Books, 1999.

———. *The Dragon Treasure of Hermes*. VT: Affinity Systems Inc., 2004.

Grant, Joan. *Winged Pharaoh*. London: Arthur Barker Ltd., 1937.

Halevi, Z'ev ben Shimon. *A Kabbalistic Universe*. Bath. UK: Gateway Books, 1993.

———. *The Anointed*. London & New York: Arkana, 1987.

———. *School of the Soul*. York Beach, ME: Weiser Books, 1986.

———. *Work of the Kabbalist*. York Beach, ME: Weiser Books, 1986.

Knight, Gareth. *Magical Images*. Oceanside, CA: Sun Chalice, 2003.

———. *The Wells of Vision*. London: SIL Trading Ltd., 2002.

Kurtz, Katherine and Deborah Turner Harris. *The Adept*. New York: Ace Books, 1991.

Regardie, Israel. *The Art of True Healing*. Novato, CA: New World Library, 1991.

CDs

Goddard, David. *Angel Workings*. vol. 1. Original music by Craig Pallet. London and Vermont, 2003.

———. *Temple of the Hidden Wisdom*. London, 2002.

Halevi, Z'ev ben Shimon. *Way of Kabbalah Meditations*. London, 2002.

ABOUT THE AUTHOR

DAVID GODDARD IS A LINEAGE-HOLDER of the Western Esoteric Tradition and trained by the spiritual master, Z'ev ben Shimon Halevi. A director of the Kabbalah Society, David is a senior teacher of Qabalah, Theurgy, and Alchemy and has written several books on these subjects: *The Sacred Magic of the Angels*, *The Tower of Alchemy*, and *The Dragon-Treasure of Hermes*.

David is also the founder of The Paros, an international School of the Soul. He teaches around the world to assist others in manifesting their innate bliss and compassion.

For details of David's ongoing work visit *www.davidgoddard.com*.

TO OUR READERS